C-4830   CAREER EXAMINATION SERIES

This is your
PASSBOOK for...

State Program Examiner II

Test Preparation Study Guide
Questions & Answers

COPYRIGHT NOTICE

This book is SOLELY intended for, is sold ONLY to, and its use is RESTRICTED to individual, bona fide applicants or candidates who qualify by virtue of having seriously filed applications for appropriate license, certificate, professional and/or promotional advancement, higher school matriculation, scholarship, or other legitimate requirements of education and/or governmental authorities.

This book is NOT intended for use, class instruction, tutoring, training, duplication, copying, reprinting, excerption, or adaptation, etc., by:

1) Other publishers
2) Proprietors and/or Instructors of "Coaching" and/or Preparatory Courses
3) Personnel and/or Training Divisions of commercial, industrial, and governmental organizations
4) Schools, colleges, or universities and/or their departments and staffs, including teachers and other personnel
5) Testing Agencies or Bureaus
6) Study groups which seek by the purchase of a single volume to copy and/or duplicate and/or adapt this material for use by the group as a whole without having purchased individual volumes for each of the members of the group
7) Et al.

Such persons would be in violation of appropriate Federal and State statutes.

PROVISION OF LICENSING AGREEMENTS – Recognized educational, commercial, industrial, and governmental institutions and organizations, and others legitimately engaged in educational pursuits, including training, testing, and measurement activities, may address request for a licensing agreement to the copyright owners, who will determine whether, and under what conditions, including fees and charges, the materials in this book may be used them. In other words, a licensing facility exists for the legitimate use of the material in this book on other than an individual basis. However, it is asseverated and affirmed here that the material in this book CANNOT be used without the receipt of the express permission of such a licensing agreement from the Publishers. Inquiries re licensing should be addressed to the company, attention rights and permissions department.

All rights reserved, including the right of reproduction in whole or in part, in any form or by any means, electronic or mechanical, including photocopying, recording, or by any information storage and retrieval system, without permission in writing from the Publisher.

Copyright © 2025 by
National Learning Corporation

212 Michael Drive, Syosset, NY 11791
(516) 921-8888 • www.passbooks.com
E-mail: info@passbooks.com

PASSBOOK® SERIES

THE *PASSBOOK® SERIES* has been created to prepare applicants and candidates for the ultimate academic battlefield – the examination room.

At some time in our lives, each and every one of us may be required to take an examination – for validation, matriculation, admission, qualification, registration, certification, or licensure.

Based on the assumption that every applicant or candidate has met the basic formal educational standards, has taken the required number of courses, and read the necessary texts, the *PASSBOOK® SERIES* furnishes the one special preparation which may assure passing with confidence, instead of failing with insecurity. Examination questions – together with answers – are furnished as the basic vehicle for study so that the mysteries of the examination and its compounding difficulties may be eliminated or diminished by a sure method.

This book is meant to help you pass your examination provided that you qualify and are serious in your objective.

The entire field is reviewed through the huge store of content information which is succinctly presented through a provocative and challenging approach – the question-and-answer method.

A climate of success is established by furnishing the correct answers at the end of each test.

You soon learn to recognize types of questions, forms of questions, and patterns of questioning. You may even begin to anticipate expected outcomes.

You perceive that many questions are repeated or adapted so that you can gain acute insights, which may enable you to score many sure points.

You learn how to confront new questions, or types of questions, and to attack them confidently and work out the correct answers.

You note objectives and emphases, and recognize pitfalls and dangers, so that you may make positive educational adjustments.

Moreover, you are kept fully informed in relation to new concepts, methods, practices, and directions in the field.

You discover that you are actually taking the examination all the time: you are preparing for the examination by "taking" an examination, not by reading extraneous and/or supererogatory textbooks.

In short, this PASSBOOK®, used directedly, should be an important factor in helping you to pass your test.

STATE PROGRAM EXAMINER II

DUTIES:
As a State Program Examiner II, you would function as examiner-in-charge of financial and performance audits and attestation engagements of State and City agencies, public benefit corporations, and for-profit and not-for-profit organizations that contract with a State agency. You would develop an audit plan or charter focusing on areas of highest risk and most significant impact; supervise performance audits in accordance with applicable standards; discuss tentative findings and recommendations with agency representatives; prepare draft audit reports covering the significant aspects of the audits; and supervise State Program Examiners I.

SCOPE OF THE EXAMINATION:
The written test is designed to test for knowledge, skills, and/or abilities in such areas as:
1. **Generally Accepted Government Auditing Standards** - These questions test for knowledge of generally accepted government auditing standards. Questions will include concepts such as planning, internal controls, audit objectives, evidence, survey work, field work, fraud, the development of findings, and audit reports. Some questions may present a situation and require candidates to apply these concepts.
2. **Supervision** - These questions test for knowledge of the principles and practices employed in planning, organizing, and controlling the activities of a work unit toward predetermined objectives. The concepts covered, usually in a situational question format, include such topics as assigning and reviewing work; evaluating performance; maintaining work standards; motivating and developing subordinates; implementing procedural change; increasing efficiency; and dealing with problems of absenteeism, morale, and discipline.
3. **Understanding and interpreting tabular material** - These questions test your ability to understand, analyze, and use the internal logic of data presented in tabular form. You may be asked to perform tasks such as completing tables, drawing conclusions from them, analyzing data trends or interrelationships, and revising or combining data sets. The concepts of rate, ratio, and proportion are tested. Mathematical operations are simple, and computational speed is not a major factor in the test.
4. **Preparing reports and official documents** - These questions test for the ability to prepare reports and other official documents for use within and among governmental agencies, in legal or regulatory settings, or for dissemination to the public. Some questions test for a knowledge of grammar, usage, punctuation, and sentence structure. Others test for the ability to present information clearly and accurately, to use the proper tone, and to organize paragraphs logically and comprehensibly.

HOW TO TAKE A TEST

I. YOU MUST PASS AN EXAMINATION

A. WHAT EVERY CANDIDATE SHOULD KNOW

Examination applicants often ask us for help in preparing for the written test. What can I study in advance? What kinds of questions will be asked? How will the test be given? How will the papers be graded?

As an applicant for a civil service examination, you may be wondering about some of these things. Our purpose here is to suggest effective methods of advance study and to describe civil service examinations.

Your chances for success on this examination can be increased if you know how to prepare. Those "pre-examination jitters" can be reduced if you know what to expect. You can even experience an adventure in good citizenship if you know why civil service exams are given.

B. WHY ARE CIVIL SERVICE EXAMINATIONS GIVEN?

Civil service examinations are important to you in two ways. As a citizen, you want public jobs filled by employees who know how to do their work. As a job seeker, you want a fair chance to compete for that job on an equal footing with other candidates. The best-known means of accomplishing this two-fold goal is the competitive examination.

Exams are widely publicized throughout the nation. They may be administered for jobs in federal, state, city, municipal, town or village governments or agencies.

Any citizen may apply, with some limitations, such as the age or residence of applicants. Your experience and education may be reviewed to see whether you meet the requirements for the particular examination. When these requirements exist, they are reasonable and applied consistently to all applicants. Thus, a competitive examination may cause you some uneasiness now, but it is your privilege and safeguard.

C. HOW ARE CIVIL SERVICE EXAMS DEVELOPED?

Examinations are carefully written by trained technicians who are specialists in the field known as "psychological measurement," in consultation with recognized authorities in the field of work that the test will cover. These experts recommend the subject matter areas or skills to be tested; only those knowledges or skills important to your success on the job are included. The most reliable books and source materials available are used as references. Together, the experts and technicians judge the difficulty level of the questions.

Test technicians know how to phrase questions so that the problem is clearly stated. Their ethics do not permit "trick" or "catch" questions. Questions may have been tried out on sample groups, or subjected to statistical analysis, to determine their usefulness.

Written tests are often used in combination with performance tests, ratings of training and experience, and oral interviews. All of these measures combine to form the best-known means of finding the right person for the right job.

II. HOW TO PASS THE WRITTEN TEST

A. NATURE OF THE EXAMINATION

To prepare intelligently for civil service examinations, you should know how they differ from school examinations you have taken. In school you were assigned certain definite pages to read or subjects to cover. The examination questions were quite detailed and usually emphasized memory. Civil service exams, on the other hand, try to discover your present ability to perform the duties of a position, plus your potentiality to learn these duties. In other words, a civil service exam attempts to predict how successful you will be. Questions cover such a broad area that they cannot be as minute and detailed as school exam questions.

In the public service similar kinds of work, or positions, are grouped together in one "class." This process is known as *position-classification*. All the positions in a class are paid according to the salary range for that class. One class title covers all of these positions, and they are all tested by the same examination.

B. FOUR BASIC STEPS

1) Study the announcement

How, then, can you know what subjects to study? Our best answer is: "Learn as much as possible about the class of positions for which you've applied." The exam will test the knowledge, skills and abilities needed to do the work.

Your most valuable source of information about the position you want is the official exam announcement. This announcement lists the training and experience qualifications. Check these standards and apply only if you come reasonably close to meeting them.

The brief description of the position in the examination announcement offers some clues to the subjects which will be tested. Think about the job itself. Review the duties in your mind. Can you perform them, or are there some in which you are rusty? Fill in the blank spots in your preparation.

Many jurisdictions preview the written test in the exam announcement by including a section called "Knowledge and Abilities Required," "Scope of the Examination," or some similar heading. Here you will find out specifically what fields will be tested.

2) Review your own background

Once you learn in general what the position is all about, and what you need to know to do the work, ask yourself which subjects you already know fairly well and which need improvement. You may wonder whether to concentrate on improving your strong areas or on building some background in your fields of weakness. When the announcement has specified "some knowledge" or "considerable knowledge," or has used adjectives like "beginning principles of..." or "advanced ... methods," you can get a clue as to the number and difficulty of questions to be asked in any given field. More questions, and hence broader coverage, would be included for those subjects which are more important in the work. Now weigh your strengths and weaknesses against the job requirements and prepare accordingly.

3) Determine the level of the position

Another way to tell how intensively you should prepare is to understand the level of the job for which you are applying. Is it the entering level? In other words, is this the position in which beginners in a field of work are hired? Or is it an intermediate or advanced level? Sometimes this is indicated by such words as "Junior" or "Senior" in the class title. Other jurisdictions use Roman numerals to designate the level – Clerk I, Clerk II, for example. The word "Supervisor" sometimes appears in the title. If the level is not indicated by the title, check the description of duties. Will you be working under very close supervision, or will you have responsibility for independent decisions in this work?

4) Choose appropriate study materials

Now that you know the subjects to be examined and the relative amount of each subject to be covered, you can choose suitable study materials. For beginning level jobs, or even advanced ones, if you have a pronounced weakness in some aspect of your training, read a modern, standard textbook in that field. Be sure it is up to date and has general coverage. Such books are normally available at your library, and the librarian will be glad to help you locate one. For entry-level positions, questions of appropriate difficulty are chosen – neither highly advanced questions, nor those too simple. Such questions require careful thought but not advanced training.

If the position for which you are applying is technical or advanced, you will read more advanced, specialized material. If you are already familiar with the basic principles of your field, elementary textbooks would waste your time. Concentrate on advanced textbooks and technical periodicals. Think through the concepts and review difficult problems in your field.

These are all general sources. You can get more ideas on your own initiative, following these leads. For example, training manuals and publications of the government agency which employs workers in your field can be useful, particularly for technical and professional positions. A letter or visit to the government department involved may result in more specific study suggestions, and certainly will provide you with a more definite idea of the exact nature of the position you are seeking.

III. KINDS OF TESTS

Tests are used for purposes other than measuring knowledge and ability to perform specified duties. For some positions, it is equally important to test ability to make adjustments to new situations or to profit from training. In others, basic mental abilities not dependent on information are essential. Questions which test these things may not appear as pertinent to the duties of the position as those which test for knowledge and information. Yet they are often highly important parts of a fair examination. For very general questions, it is almost impossible to help you direct your study efforts. What we can do is to point out some of the more common of these general abilities needed in public service positions and describe some typical questions.

1) General information

Broad, general information has been found useful for predicting job success in some kinds of work. This is tested in a variety of ways, from vocabulary lists to questions about current events. Basic background in some field of work, such as sociology or economics, may be sampled in a group of questions. Often these are principles which have become familiar to most persons through exposure rather than through formal training. It is difficult to advise you how to study for these questions; being alert to the world around you is our best suggestion.

2) Verbal ability

An example of an ability needed in many positions is verbal or language ability. Verbal ability is, in brief, the ability to use and understand words. Vocabulary and grammar tests are typical measures of this ability. Reading comprehension or paragraph interpretation questions are common in many kinds of civil service tests. You are given a paragraph of written material and asked to find its central meaning.

3) Numerical ability

Number skills can be tested by the familiar arithmetic problem, by checking paired lists of numbers to see which are alike and which are different, or by interpreting charts and graphs. In the latter test, a graph may be printed in the test booklet which you are asked to use as the basis for answering questions.

4) Observation

A popular test for law-enforcement positions is the observation test. A picture is shown to you for several minutes, then taken away. Questions about the picture test your ability to observe both details and larger elements.

5) Following directions

In many positions in the public service, the employee must be able to carry out written instructions dependably and accurately. You may be given a chart with several columns, each column listing a variety of information. The questions require you to carry out directions involving the information given in the chart.

6) Skills and aptitudes

Performance tests effectively measure some manual skills and aptitudes. When the skill is one in which you are trained, such as typing or shorthand, you can practice. These tests are often very much like those given in business school or high school courses. For many of the other skills and aptitudes, however, no short-time preparation can be made. Skills and abilities natural to you or that you have developed throughout your lifetime are being tested.

Many of the general questions just described provide all the data needed to answer the questions and ask you to use your reasoning ability to find the answers. Your best preparation for these tests, as well as for tests of facts and ideas, is to be at your physical and mental best. You, no doubt, have your own methods of getting into an exam-taking mood and keeping "in shape." The next section lists some ideas on this subject.

IV. KINDS OF QUESTIONS

Only rarely is the "essay" question, which you answer in narrative form, used in civil service tests. Civil service tests are usually of the short-answer type. Full instructions for answering these questions will be given to you at the examination. But in case this is your first experience with short-answer questions and separate answer sheets, here is what you need to know:

1) Multiple-choice Questions

Most popular of the short-answer questions is the "multiple choice" or "best answer" question. It can be used, for example, to test for factual knowledge, ability to solve problems or judgment in meeting situations found at work.

A multiple-choice question is normally one of three types—
- It can begin with an incomplete statement followed by several possible endings. You are to find the one ending which *best* completes the statement, although some of the others may not be entirely wrong.
- It can also be a complete statement in the form of a question which is answered by choosing one of the statements listed.

- It can be in the form of a problem – again you select the best answer.

Here is an example of a multiple-choice question with a discussion which should give you some clues as to the method for choosing the right answer:

When an employee has a complaint about his assignment, the action which will *best* help him overcome his difficulty is to
A. discuss his difficulty with his coworkers
B. take the problem to the head of the organization
C. take the problem to the person who gave him the assignment
D. say nothing to anyone about his complaint

In answering this question, you should study each of the choices to find which is best. Consider choice "A" – Certainly an employee may discuss his complaint with fellow employees, but no change or improvement can result, and the complaint remains unresolved. Choice "B" is a poor choice since the head of the organization probably does not know what assignment you have been given, and taking your problem to him is known as "going over the head" of the supervisor. The supervisor, or person who made the assignment, is the person who can clarify it or correct any injustice. Choice "C" is, therefore, correct. To say nothing, as in choice "D," is unwise. Supervisors have and interest in knowing the problems employees are facing, and the employee is seeking a solution to his problem.

2) True/False Questions

The "true/false" or "right/wrong" form of question is sometimes used. Here a complete statement is given. Your job is to decide whether the statement is right or wrong.

SAMPLE: A roaming cell-phone call to a nearby city costs less than a non-roaming call to a distant city.

This statement is wrong, or false, since roaming calls are more expensive.

This is not a complete list of all possible question forms, although most of the others are variations of these common types. You will always get complete directions for answering questions. Be sure you understand *how* to mark your answers – ask questions until you do.

V. RECORDING YOUR ANSWERS

Computer terminals are used more and more today for many different kinds of exams.
For an examination with very few applicants, you may be told to record your answers in the test booklet itself. Separate answer sheets are much more common. If this separate answer sheet is to be scored by machine – and this is often the case – it is highly important that you mark your answers correctly in order to get credit.
An electronic scoring machine is often used in civil service offices because of the speed with which papers can be scored. Machine-scored answer sheets must be marked with a pencil, which will be given to you. This pencil has a high graphite content which responds to the electronic scoring machine. As a matter of fact, stray dots may register as answers, so do not let your pencil rest on the answer sheet while you are pondering the correct answer. Also, if your pencil lead breaks or is otherwise defective, ask for another.

Since the answer sheet will be dropped in a slot in the scoring machine, be careful not to bend the corners or get the paper crumpled.

The answer sheet normally has five vertical columns of numbers, with 30 numbers to a column. These numbers correspond to the question numbers in your test booklet. After each number, going across the page are four or five pairs of dotted lines. These short dotted lines have small letters or numbers above them. The first two pairs may also have a "T" or "F" above the letters. This indicates that the first two pairs only are to be used if the questions are of the true-false type. If the questions are multiple choice, disregard the "T" and "F" and pay attention only to the small letters or numbers.

Answer your questions in the manner of the sample that follows:

32. The largest city in the United States is
   A. Washington, D.C.
   B. New York City
   C. Chicago
   D. Detroit
   E. San Francisco

1) Choose the answer you think is best. (New York City is the largest, so "B" is correct.)
2) Find the row of dotted lines numbered the same as the question you are answering. (Find row number 32)
3) Find the pair of dotted lines corresponding to the answer. (Find the pair of lines under the mark "B.")
4) Make a solid black mark between the dotted lines.

VI. BEFORE THE TEST

Common sense will help you find procedures to follow to get ready for an examination. Too many of us, however, overlook these sensible measures. Indeed, nervousness and fatigue have been found to be the most serious reasons why applicants fail to do their best on civil service tests. Here is a list of reminders:

- Begin your preparation early – Don't wait until the last minute to go scurrying around for books and materials or to find out what the position is all about.
- Prepare continuously – An hour a night for a week is better than an all-night cram session. This has been definitely established. What is more, a night a week for a month will return better dividends than crowding your study into a shorter period of time.
- Locate the place of the exam – You have been sent a notice telling you when and where to report for the examination. If the location is in a different town or otherwise unfamiliar to you, it would be well to inquire the best route and learn something about the building.
- Relax the night before the test – Allow your mind to rest. Do not study at all that night. Plan some mild recreation or diversion; then go to bed early and get a good night's sleep.
- Get up early enough to make a leisurely trip to the place for the test – This way unforeseen events, traffic snarls, unfamiliar buildings, etc. will not upset you.
- Dress comfortably – A written test is not a fashion show. You will be known by number and not by name, so wear something comfortable.

- Leave excess paraphernalia at home – Shopping bags and odd bundles will get in your way. You need bring only the items mentioned in the official notice you received; usually everything you need is provided. Do not bring reference books to the exam. They will only confuse those last minutes and be taken away from you when in the test room.
- Arrive somewhat ahead of time – If because of transportation schedules you must get there very early, bring a newspaper or magazine to take your mind off yourself while waiting.
- Locate the examination room – When you have found the proper room, you will be directed to the seat or part of the room where you will sit. Sometimes you are given a sheet of instructions to read while you are waiting. Do not fill out any forms until you are told to do so; just read them and be prepared.
- Relax and prepare to listen to the instructions
- If you have any physical problem that may keep you from doing your best, be sure to tell the test administrator. If you are sick or in poor health, you really cannot do your best on the exam. You can come back and take the test some other time.

VII. AT THE TEST

The day of the test is here and you have the test booklet in your hand. The temptation to get going is very strong. Caution! There is more to success than knowing the right answers. You must know how to identify your papers and understand variations in the type of short-answer question used in this particular examination. Follow these suggestions for maximum results from your efforts:

1) Cooperate with the monitor
The test administrator has a duty to create a situation in which you can be as much at ease as possible. He will give instructions, tell you when to begin, check to see that you are marking your answer sheet correctly, and so on. He is not there to guard you, although he will see that your competitors do not take unfair advantage. He wants to help you do your best.

2) Listen to all instructions
Don't jump the gun! Wait until you understand all directions. In most civil service tests you get more time than you need to answer the questions. So don't be in a hurry. Read each word of instructions until you clearly understand the meaning. Study the examples, listen to all announcements and follow directions. Ask questions if you do not understand what to do.

3) Identify your papers
Civil service exams are usually identified by number only. You will be assigned a number; you must not put your name on your test papers. Be sure to copy your number correctly. Since more than one exam may be given, copy your exact examination title.

4) Plan your time
Unless you are told that a test is a "speed" or "rate of work" test, speed itself is usually not important. Time enough to answer all the questions will be provided, but this does not mean that you have all day. An overall time limit has been set. Divide the total time (in minutes) by the number of questions to determine the approximate time you have for each question.

5) Do not linger over difficult questions

If you come across a difficult question, mark it with a paper clip (useful to have along) and come back to it when you have been through the booklet. One caution if you do this – be sure to skip a number on your answer sheet as well. Check often to be sure that you have not lost your place and that you are marking in the row numbered the same as the question you are answering.

6) Read the questions

Be sure you know what the question asks! Many capable people are unsuccessful because they failed to *read* the questions correctly.

7) Answer all questions

Unless you have been instructed that a penalty will be deducted for incorrect answers, it is better to guess than to omit a question.

8) Speed tests

It is often better NOT to guess on speed tests. It has been found that on timed tests people are tempted to spend the last few seconds before time is called in marking answers at random – without even reading them – in the hope of picking up a few extra points. To discourage this practice, the instructions may warn you that your score will be "corrected" for guessing. That is, a penalty will be applied. The incorrect answers will be deducted from the correct ones, or some other penalty formula will be used.

9) Review your answers

If you finish before time is called, go back to the questions you guessed or omitted to give them further thought. Review other answers if you have time.

10) Return your test materials

If you are ready to leave before others have finished or time is called, take ALL your materials to the monitor and leave quietly. Never take any test material with you. The monitor can discover whose papers are not complete, and taking a test booklet may be grounds for disqualification.

VIII. EXAMINATION TECHNIQUES

1) Read the general instructions carefully. These are usually printed on the first page of the exam booklet. As a rule, these instructions refer to the timing of the examination; the fact that you should not start work until the signal and must stop work at a signal, etc. If there are any *special* instructions, such as a choice of questions to be answered, make sure that you note this instruction carefully.

2) When you are ready to start work on the examination, that is as soon as the signal has been given, read the instructions to each question booklet, underline any key words or phrases, such as *least, best, outline, describe* and the like. In this way you will tend to answer as requested rather than discover on reviewing your paper that you *listed without describing*, that you selected the *worst* choice rather than the *best* choice, etc.

3) If the examination is of the objective or multiple-choice type – that is, each question will also give a series of possible answers: A, B, C or D, and you are called upon to select the best answer and write the letter next to that answer on your answer paper – it is advisable to start answering each question in turn. There may be anywhere from 50 to 100 such questions in the three or four hours allotted and you can see how much time would be taken if you read through all the questions before beginning to answer any. Furthermore, if you come across a question or group of questions which you know would be difficult to answer, it would undoubtedly affect your handling of all the other questions.

4) If the examination is of the essay type and contains but a few questions, it is a moot point as to whether you should read all the questions before starting to answer any one. Of course, if you are given a choice – say five out of seven and the like – then it is essential to read all the questions so you can eliminate the two that are most difficult. If, however, you are asked to answer all the questions, there may be danger in trying to answer the easiest one first because you may find that you will spend too much time on it. The best technique is to answer the first question, then proceed to the second, etc.

5) Time your answers. Before the exam begins, write down the time it started, then add the time allowed for the examination and write down the time it must be completed, then divide the time available somewhat as follows:
    - If 3-1/2 hours are allowed, that would be 210 minutes. If you have 80 objective-type questions, that would be an average of 2-1/2 minutes per question. Allow yourself no more than 2 minutes per question, or a total of 160 minutes, which will permit about 50 minutes to review.
    - If for the time allotment of 210 minutes there are 7 essay questions to answer, that would average about 30 minutes a question. Give yourself only 25 minutes per question so that you have about 35 minutes to review.

6) The most important instruction is to *read each question* and make sure you know what is wanted. The second most important instruction is to *time yourself properly* so that you answer every question. The third most important instruction is to *answer every question*. Guess if you have to but include something for each question. Remember that you will receive no credit for a blank and will probably receive some credit if you write something in answer to an essay question. If you guess a letter – say "B" for a multiple-choice question – you may have guessed right. If you leave a blank as an answer to a multiple-choice question, the examiners may respect your feelings but it will not add a point to your score. Some exams may penalize you for wrong answers, so in such cases *only*, you may not want to guess unless you have some basis for your answer.

7) Suggestions
    a. Objective-type questions
        1. Examine the question booklet for proper sequence of pages and questions
        2. Read all instructions carefully
        3. Skip any question which seems too difficult; return to it after all other questions have been answered
        4. Apportion your time properly; do not spend too much time on any single question or group of questions

5. Note and underline key words – *all, most, fewest, least, best, worst, same, opposite,* etc.
6. Pay particular attention to negatives
7. Note unusual option, e.g., unduly long, short, complex, different or similar in content to the body of the question
8. Observe the use of "hedging" words – *probably, may, most likely,* etc.
9. Make sure that your answer is put next to the same number as the question
10. Do not second-guess unless you have good reason to believe the second answer is definitely more correct
11. Cross out original answer if you decide another answer is more accurate; do not erase until you are ready to hand your paper in
12. Answer all questions; guess unless instructed otherwise
13. Leave time for review

    b. Essay questions
      1. Read each question carefully
      2. Determine exactly what is wanted. Underline key words or phrases.
      3. Decide on outline or paragraph answer
      4. Include many different points and elements unless asked to develop any one or two points or elements
      5. Show impartiality by giving pros and cons unless directed to select one side only
      6. Make and write down any assumptions you find necessary to answer the questions
      7. Watch your English, grammar, punctuation and choice of words
      8. Time your answers; don't crowd material

8) Answering the essay question

Most essay questions can be answered by framing the specific response around several key words or ideas. Here are a few such key words or ideas:

M's: manpower, materials, methods, money, management
P's: purpose, program, policy, plan, procedure, practice, problems, pitfalls, personnel, public relations

    a. Six basic steps in handling problems:
      1. Preliminary plan and background development
      2. Collect information, data and facts
      3. Analyze and interpret information, data and facts
      4. Analyze and develop solutions as well as make recommendations
      5. Prepare report and sell recommendations
      6. Install recommendations and follow up effectiveness

    b. Pitfalls to avoid
      1. *Taking things for granted* – A statement of the situation does not necessarily imply that each of the elements is necessarily true; for example, a complaint may be invalid and biased so that all that can be taken for granted is that a complaint has been registered

2. *Considering only one side of a situation* – Wherever possible, indicate several alternatives and then point out the reasons you selected the best one
3. *Failing to indicate follow up* – Whenever your answer indicates action on your part, make certain that you will take proper follow-up action to see how successful your recommendations, procedures or actions turn out to be
4. *Taking too long in answering any single question* – Remember to time your answers properly

IX. AFTER THE TEST

Scoring procedures differ in detail among civil service jurisdictions although the general principles are the same. Whether the papers are hand-scored or graded by machine we have described, they are nearly always graded by number. That is, the person who marks the paper knows only the number – never the name – of the applicant. Not until all the papers have been graded will they be matched with names. If other tests, such as training and experience or oral interview ratings have been given, scores will be combined. Different parts of the examination usually have different weights. For example, the written test might count 60 percent of the final grade, and a rating of training and experience 40 percent. In many jurisdictions, veterans will have a certain number of points added to their grades.

After the final grade has been determined, the names are placed in grade order and an eligible list is established. There are various methods for resolving ties between those who get the same final grade – probably the most common is to place first the name of the person whose application was received first. Job offers are made from the eligible list in the order the names appear on it. You will be notified of your grade and your rank as soon as all these computations have been made. This will be done as rapidly as possible.

People who are found to meet the requirements in the announcement are called "eligibles." Their names are put on a list of eligible candidates. An eligible's chances of getting a job depend on how high he stands on this list and how fast agencies are filling jobs from the list.

When a job is to be filled from a list of eligibles, the agency asks for the names of people on the list of eligibles for that job. When the civil service commission receives this request, it sends to the agency the names of the three people highest on this list. Or, if the job to be filled has specialized requirements, the office sends the agency the names of the top three persons who meet these requirements from the general list.

The appointing officer makes a choice from among the three people whose names were sent to him. If the selected person accepts the appointment, the names of the others are put back on the list to be considered for future openings.

That is the rule in hiring from all kinds of eligible lists, whether they are for typist, carpenter, chemist, or something else. For every vacancy, the appointing officer has his choice of any one of the top three eligibles on the list. This explains why the person whose name is on top of the list sometimes does not get an appointment when some of the persons lower on the list do. If the appointing officer chooses the second or third eligible, the No. 1 eligible does not get a job at once, but stays on the list until he is appointed or the list is terminated.

X. HOW TO PASS THE INTERVIEW TEST

The examination for which you applied requires an oral interview test. You have already taken the written test and you are now being called for the interview test – the final part of the formal examination.

You may think that it is not possible to prepare for an interview test and that there are no procedures to follow during an interview. Our purpose is to point out some things you can do in advance that will help you and some good rules to follow and pitfalls to avoid while you are being interviewed.

What is an interview supposed to test?

The written examination is designed to test the technical knowledge and competence of the candidate; the oral is designed to evaluate intangible qualities, not readily measured otherwise, and to establish a list showing the relative fitness of each candidate – as measured against his competitors – for the position sought. Scoring is not on the basis of "right" and "wrong," but on a sliding scale of values ranging from "not passable" to "outstanding." As a matter of fact, it is possible to achieve a relatively low score without a single "incorrect" answer because of evident weakness in the qualities being measured.

Occasionally, an examination may consist entirely of an oral test – either an individual or a group oral. In such cases, information is sought concerning the technical knowledges and abilities of the candidate, since there has been no written examination for this purpose. More commonly, however, an oral test is used to supplement a written examination.

Who conducts interviews?

The composition of oral boards varies among different jurisdictions. In nearly all, a representative of the personnel department serves as chairman. One of the members of the board may be a representative of the department in which the candidate would work. In some cases, "outside experts" are used, and, frequently, a businessman or some other representative of the general public is asked to serve. Labor and management or other special groups may be represented. The aim is to secure the services of experts in the appropriate field.

However the board is composed, it is a good idea (and not at all improper or unethical) to ascertain in advance of the interview who the members are and what groups they represent. When you are introduced to them, you will have some idea of their backgrounds and interests, and at least you will not stutter and stammer over their names.

What should be done before the interview?

While knowledge about the board members is useful and takes some of the surprise element out of the interview, there is other preparation which is more substantive. It *is* possible to prepare for an oral interview – in several ways:

1) Keep a copy of your application and review it carefully before the interview

This may be the only document before the oral board, and the starting point of the interview. Know what education and experience you have listed there, and the sequence and dates of all of it. Sometimes the board will ask you to review the highlights of your experience for them; you should not have to hem and haw doing it.

2) Study the class specification and the examination announcement

Usually, the oral board has one or both of these to guide them. The qualities, characteristics or knowledges required by the position sought are stated in these documents. They offer valuable clues as to the nature of the oral interview. For example, if the job involves supervisory responsibilities, the announcement will usually indicate that knowledge of modern supervisory methods and the qualifications of the candidate as a supervisor will be tested. If so, you can expect such questions, frequently in the form of a hypothetical situation which you are expected to solve. NEVER go into an oral without knowledge of the duties and responsibilities of the job you seek.

3) Think through each qualification required

Try to visualize the kind of questions you would ask if you were a board member. How well could you answer them? Try especially to appraise your own knowledge and background in each area, *measured against the job sought*, and identify any areas in which you are weak. Be critical and realistic – do not flatter yourself.

4) Do some general reading in areas in which you feel you may be weak

For example, if the job involves supervision and your past experience has NOT, some general reading in supervisory methods and practices, particularly in the field of human relations, might be useful. Do NOT study agency procedures or detailed manuals. The oral board will be testing your understanding and capacity, not your memory.

5) Get a good night's sleep and watch your general health and mental attitude

You will want a clear head at the interview. Take care of a cold or any other minor ailment, and of course, no hangovers.

What should be done on the day of the interview?

Now comes the day of the interview itself. Give yourself plenty of time to get there. Plan to arrive somewhat ahead of the scheduled time, particularly if your appointment is in the fore part of the day. If a previous candidate fails to appear, the board might be ready for you a bit early. By early afternoon an oral board is almost invariably behind schedule if there are many candidates, and you may have to wait. Take along a book or magazine to read, or your application to review, but leave any extraneous material in the waiting room when you go in for your interview. In any event, relax and compose yourself.

The matter of dress is important. The board is forming impressions about you – from your experience, your manners, your attitude, and your appearance. Give your personal appearance careful attention. Dress your best, but not your flashiest. Choose conservative, appropriate clothing, and be sure it is immaculate. This is a business interview, and your appearance should indicate that you regard it as such. Besides, being well groomed and properly dressed will help boost your confidence.

Sooner or later, someone will call your name and escort you into the interview room. *This is it.* From here on you are on your own. It is too late for any more preparation. But remember, you asked for this opportunity to prove your fitness, and you are here because your request was granted.

What happens when you go in?

The usual sequence of events will be as follows: The clerk (who is often the board stenographer) will introduce you to the chairman of the oral board, who will introduce you to the other members of the board. Acknowledge the introductions before you sit down. Do not be surprised if you find a microphone facing you or a stenotypist sitting by. Oral interviews are usually recorded in the event of an appeal or other review.

Usually the chairman of the board will open the interview by reviewing the highlights of your education and work experience from your application – primarily for the benefit of the other members of the board, as well as to get the material into the record. Do not interrupt or comment unless there is an error or significant misinterpretation; if that is the case, do not hesitate. But do not quibble about insignificant matters. Also, he will usually ask you some question about your education, experience or your present job – partly to get you to start talking and to establish the interviewing "rapport." He may start the actual questioning, or turn it over to one of the other members. Frequently, each member undertakes the questioning on a particular area, one in which he is perhaps most competent, so you can expect each member to participate in the examination. Because time is limited, you may also expect some rather abrupt switches in the direction the questioning takes, so do not be upset by it. Normally, a board member will not pursue a single line of questioning unless he discovers a particular strength or weakness.

After each member has participated, the chairman will usually ask whether any member has any further questions, then will ask you if you have anything you wish to add. Unless you are expecting this question, it may floor you. Worse, it may start you off on an extended, extemporaneous speech. The board is not usually seeking more information. The question is principally to offer you a last opportunity to present further qualifications or to indicate that you have nothing to add. So, if you feel that a significant qualification or characteristic has been overlooked, it is proper to point it out in a sentence or so. Do not compliment the board on the thoroughness of their examination – they have been sketchy, and you know it. If you wish, merely say, "No thank you, I have nothing further to add." This is a point where you can "talk yourself out" of a good impression or fail to present an important bit of information. Remember, *you close the interview yourself.*

The chairman will then say, "That is all, Mr. _____, thank you." Do not be startled; the interview is over, and quicker than you think. Thank him, gather your belongings and take your leave. Save your sigh of relief for the other side of the door.

How to put your best foot forward

Throughout this entire process, you may feel that the board individually and collectively is trying to pierce your defenses, seek out your hidden weaknesses and embarrass and confuse you. Actually, this is not true. They are obliged to make an appraisal of your qualifications for the job you are seeking, and they want to see you in your best light. Remember, they must interview all candidates and a non-cooperative candidate may become a failure in spite of their best efforts to bring out his qualifications. Here are 15 suggestions that will help you:

1) Be natural – Keep your attitude confident, not cocky

If you are not confident that you can do the job, do not expect the board to be. Do not apologize for your weaknesses, try to bring out your strong points. The board is interested in a positive, not negative, presentation. Cockiness will antagonize any board member and make him wonder if you are covering up a weakness by a false show of strength.

2) Get comfortable, but don't lounge or sprawl

Sit erectly but not stiffly. A careless posture may lead the board to conclude that you are careless in other things, or at least that you are not impressed by the importance of the occasion. Either conclusion is natural, even if incorrect. Do not fuss with your clothing, a pencil or an ashtray. Your hands may occasionally be useful to emphasize a point; do not let them become a point of distraction.

3) Do not wisecrack or make small talk

This is a serious situation, and your attitude should show that you consider it as such. Further, the time of the board is limited – they do not want to waste it, and neither should you.

4) Do not exaggerate your experience or abilities
In the first place, from information in the application or other interviews and sources, the board may know more about you than you think. Secondly, you probably will not get away with it. An experienced board is rather adept at spotting such a situation, so do not take the chance.

5) If you know a board member, do not make a point of it, yet do not hide it
Certainly you are not fooling him, and probably not the other members of the board. Do not try to take advantage of your acquaintanceship – it will probably do you little good.

6) Do not dominate the interview
Let the board do that. They will give you the clues – do not assume that you have to do all the talking. Realize that the board has a number of questions to ask you, and do not try to take up all the interview time by showing off your extensive knowledge of the answer to the first one.

7) Be attentive
You only have 20 minutes or so, and you should keep your attention at its sharpest throughout. When a member is addressing a problem or question to you, give him your undivided attention. Address your reply principally to him, but do not exclude the other board members.

8) Do not interrupt
A board member may be stating a problem for you to analyze. He will ask you a question when the time comes. Let him state the problem, and wait for the question.

9) Make sure you understand the question
Do not try to answer until you are sure what the question is. If it is not clear, restate it in your own words or ask the board member to clarify it for you. However, do not haggle about minor elements.

10) Reply promptly but not hastily
A common entry on oral board rating sheets is "candidate responded readily," or "candidate hesitated in replies." Respond as promptly and quickly as you can, but do not jump to a hasty, ill-considered answer.

11) Do not be peremptory in your answers
A brief answer is proper – but do not fire your answer back. That is a losing game from your point of view. The board member can probably ask questions much faster than you can answer them.

12) Do not try to create the answer you think the board member wants
He is interested in what kind of mind you have and how it works – not in playing games. Furthermore, he can usually spot this practice and will actually grade you down on it.

13) Do not switch sides in your reply merely to agree with a board member
Frequently, a member will take a contrary position merely to draw you out and to see if you are willing and able to defend your point of view. Do not start a debate, yet do not surrender a good position. If a position is worth taking, it is worth defending.

14) Do not be afraid to admit an error in judgment if you are shown to be wrong

The board knows that you are forced to reply without any opportunity for careful consideration. Your answer may be demonstrably wrong. If so, admit it and get on with the interview.

15) Do not dwell at length on your present job

The opening question may relate to your present assignment. Answer the question but do not go into an extended discussion. You are being examined for a *new* job, not your present one. As a matter of fact, try to phrase ALL your answers in terms of the job for which you are being examined.

Basis of Rating

Probably you will forget most of these "do's" and "don'ts" when you walk into the oral interview room. Even remembering them all will not ensure you a passing grade. Perhaps you did not have the qualifications in the first place. But remembering them will help you to put your best foot forward, without treading on the toes of the board members.

Rumor and popular opinion to the contrary notwithstanding, an oral board wants you to make the best appearance possible. They know you are under pressure – but they also want to see how you respond to it as a guide to what your reaction would be under the pressures of the job you seek. They will be influenced by the degree of poise you display, the personal traits you show and the manner in which you respond.

ABOUT THIS BOOK

This book contains tests divided into Examination Sections. Go through each test, answering every question in the margin. We have also attached a sample answer sheet at the back of the book that can be removed and used. At the end of each test look at the answer key and check your answers. On the ones you got wrong, look at the right answer choice and learn. Do not fill in the answers first. Do not memorize the questions and answers, but understand the answer and principles involved. On your test, the questions will likely be different from the samples. Questions are changed and new ones added. If you understand these past questions you should have success with any changes that arise. Tests may consist of several types of questions. We have additional books on each subject should more study be advisable or necessary for you. Finally, the more you study, the better prepared you will be. This book is intended to be the last thing you study before you walk into the examination room. Prior study of relevant texts is also recommended. NLC publishes some of these in our Fundamental Series. Knowledge and good sense are important factors in passing your exam. Good luck also helps. So now study this Passbook, absorb the material contained within and take that knowledge into the examination. Then do your best to pass that exam.

EXAMINATION SECTION

EXAMINATION SECTION

TEST 1

DIRECTIONS: Each question or incomplete statement is followed by several suggested answers or completions. Select the one that BEST answers the question or completes the statement. *PRINT THE LETTER OF THE CORRECT ANSWER IN THE SPACE AT THE RIGHT.*

1. The Donaldson Company's cash balance includes a sum of $1,200,000 appropriated by the Board of Directors for the purchase of new equipment. On its financial statements, this amount should be included on the
   A. balance sheet as a current asset
   B. balance sheet as a non-current asset, specifically identified
   C. balance sheet as a fixed asset, included as part of plant cost
   D. income statement as a non-operating expense

   1.____

2. The trial balance of the Davis Corporation as of June 30, 2021, the end of its fiscal year, included opposite the title ESTIMATED FEDERAL INCOME TAXES ACCRUED the amount of $35,000, which included the company's estimate of the Federal income tax it would have to pay for its 2021 fiscal year and the amount of an unpaid additional assessment for the 2018 fiscal year.
   This amount should appear on the balance sheet as a(n)
   A. general reserve   B. reduction of current assets
   C. current liability   D. allocation of retained income

   2.____

3. A weekly payroll check was issued to an hourly employee based upon 88 hours of work instead of the normal 38 hours. The time card was somewhat illegible, and the number looked like it could have been 88.
   The BEST control procedure to prevent such an error would be
   A. desk checking   B. a hash total
   C. a limit test   D. a code check

   3.____

4. In preparing a bank reconciliation, outstanding checks should be
   A. *deducted* from the balance per books
   B. *deducted* from the balance per bank statement
   C. *added* to the balance per books
   D. *added* to the balance per bank statement

   4.____

5. Independence is essential and is expected under the generally accepted auditing standards.
   The face and appearance of integrity and objectivity are BEST maintained if
   A. the auditor is unbiased
   B. the auditor is aware of the problem of third party liability
   C. there is no financial relationship between the client and the auditor
   D. all financial relationships between the auditor and the client are reported in footnote form

   5.____

6. An audit program is a plan of action and is used to guide the auditor in planning his work.
   Such a program, if standardized, must be modified to
   A. observe limits that management places on the audit
   B. counteract internal control weaknesses
   C. meet the limited training of the auditor
   D. limit interference with work of the firm being audited

6.____

7. In auditing the *Owner's Equity* section of any company, the section related to a publicly-held corporation which uses a transfer agent and registrar would be more intricate than the audit of a partnership.
   Therefore, the procedure that an auditor should use in this case is to
   A. obtain a listing of the number of shares of securities outstanding
   B. make a count of the number of shareholders
   C. determine that all stock transfers have been properly handled
   D. count the number of shares of stock in the treasury

7.____

8. In recent years, it has become increasingly more important to determine the correct number of shares outstanding when auditing the owner's equity accounts.
   This is TRUE because
   A. there has been more fraud with respect to securities issued
   B. there are increased complexities determining the earnings per share
   C. there are more large corporations
   D. the auditor has to test the amount of invested capital

8.____

9. In auditing corporation records, an auditor must refer to some corporate documents that are not accounting documents.
   The one of the following to which he is LEAST likely to refer is
   A. minutes of the board of directors meeting
   B. articles of incorporation of the corporation
   C. correspondence with public relations firms and the shareholders
   D. the by-laws of the corporation

9.____

10. A generally accepted auditing procedure which has been required by AICPA requirements is the observation of inventories.
    Since it is impossible to observe the entire inventory of a large firm, the auditor may satisfy this requirement by
    A. establishing the balance by the use of a gross profit percentage method
    B. using sampling procedures to verify the count made by the client
    C. accepting the perpetual inventory records, once he has established that the entries are arithmetically accurate
    D. accepting the management statement that the inventory is correct as to quantity where observation is difficult

10.____

11. Materiality is an important consideration in all aspects of an audit examination. Attention must be given to accounts with small and zero balances when examining accounts payable.
    This does not conflict with the concept of materiality because

11.____

A. The size of a balance is no clue to possible understatement of a liability
B. the balance of the account is not a measure of materiality
C. a sampling technique may suggest examining those accounts under consideration
D. the total of the accounts payable may be a material amount and, therefore, no individual account payable should be eliminated from review

12. In establishing the amount of a liability recorded on the books, which of the following types of evidence should an auditor consider to be the MOST reliable?
    A. A check issued by the company and bearing the payee's endorsement which is included with the bank statement
    B. Confirmation of an account payable balance mailed by and returned directly to the auditor
    C. A sales invoice issued by the client with a delivery receipt from an outside trucker attached
    D. A working paper prepared by the client's accountant and reviewed by the client's controller

12.____

13. Prior period adjustments as defined by APIB Opinion #9 issued by the AICPA never flow through the income statement.
The one of the following which is NOT one of the four criteria established b APB #9 for meeting the qualifications for treatment as a prior period adjustment is that the adjustment item
    A. is not susceptible to reasonable extension prior to the current period
    B. must be determined primarily by someone other than company management
    C. can be specifically identified with and directly related to the business activities of a particular prior period
    D. when placed in the current period would give undesirable results of operations

13.____

14. The subject caption which does NOT belong in a report of a financial audit and review of operations of public agency is
    A. Audit Program
    B. Description of Agency Organization and Function
    C. Summary Statement of Findings
    D. Details of Findings

14.____

15. At the inception of an audit of a public assistance agency, you ascertain that the one-year period of your audit includes 240,000 serially numbered payment vouchers.
The sample selection which would enable you to render the MOST generally acceptable opinion on the number of ineligible persons receiving public assistance is
    A. the number of vouchers issued in a one-month period
    B. every hundredth voucher
    C. a random statistical selection
    D. an equal size block of vouchers from each month

15.____

16. Of the following, the one which BEST describes an internal control system is the
    A. division of the handling and recording of each transaction into component parts so as to involve at least two persons, with each performing an unduplicated part of each transaction
    B. expansion of the worksheet to include provisions for adjustments to the books of account prior to preparation of the financial statements
    C. recording of transactions affecting negotiable instruments in accordance with the principles of debit and credit, and giving these instruments special treatment if they are interest or non-interest bearing notes
    D. taking of discounts, when properly authorized by the vendor, as an incentive for prompt payment

17. During audits of small businesses, an accountant is less likely to find that these establishments have a system of internal control comparable to larger firms because small businesses GENERALLY
    A. can absorb the cost of small fraudulent acts which may be perpetrated
    B. benefit more than larger firms by prevention of fraud than by detection of fraud
    C. have limited staff and the costs of maintaining the system are high
    D. use a double entry system which serves as a substitute for internal control

18. In the performance of a financial audit, especially one where there is a need for a thorough knowledge of law, an accountant would BEST be advised to
    A. rely on the testimony of witnesses, as they may be found during the course of the audit, in preference to the written record
    B. rely on the presumption that the client's actions are illegal when the audit discloses meager facts or evidence
    C. be aware of the specific legal objectives he is attempting to attain by means of his audit
    D. be aware of different conclusions he can reach depending upon what facts are stressed or discounted in his audit

19. There are various types of budgets which are used to measure different government activities.
    The type of budget which PARTICULARLY measures input of resource as compared with output service is the _____ budget.
    A. capital   B. traditional   C. performance   D. program

20. Bank balances are usually confirmed through the use of a standard bank confirmation form as authorized by the AICPA and the Bank Administration Institute.
    In addition to bank balances, these confirmations ALSO confirm
    A. the credit rating of the client
    B. details of all deposits during the past month
    C. loans and contingent liabilities outstanding
    D. securities held by the bank as custodian or the client

KEY (CORRECT ANSWERS)

1.	B	11.	A
2.	C	12.	B
3.	C	13.	D
4.	B	14.	A
5.	C	15.	C
6.	B	16.	A
7.	A	17.	C
8.	B	18.	C
9.	C	19.	C
10.	B	20.	C

TEST 2

DIRECTIONS: Each question or incomplete statement is followed by several suggested answers or completions. Select the one that BEST answers the question or completes the statement. *PRINT THE LETTER OF THE CORRECT ANSWER IN THE SPACE AT THE RIGHT.*

Questions 1-3.

DIRECTIONS: Questions 1 through 3 are based on the classification of items into the appropriate section of a corporation balance sheet. The list of sections to be used is given below:

    Current Assets   Investments
    Current Liabilities   Long-term Liabilities
    Deferred Credits   Paid-in Capital
    Deferred Expenses   Plant Assets
    Intangible assets   Retained Earnings

1. With respect to *Bonds Payable Due* in 2021, the PROPER classification is
   A. Investments
   B. Paid-in Capital
   C. Retained Earnings
   D. Long-term Liabilities

2. With respect to *Premium on Common Stock*, the PROPER classification is
   A. Intangible Assets
   B. Investments
   C. Retained Earnings
   D. Paid-in Capital

3. With respect to *Organization Costs,* the PROPER classification is
   A. Intangible Assets
   B. Investments
   C. Plant Assets
   D. Current Liabilities

4. J. Frost operates a small, individually owned repair service and maintains adequate double entry records. A review of his bank accounts and other available financial records yields the following information:
   Deposits made during 2021 per bank statements totaled $360,000. Deposits included a bank loan of $25,000 and an additional investment by Frost of $5,000. Disbursements during 2021 per bank statements totaled $305,000. This amount includes personal withdrawals of $28,500 and repayment of debt of $15,000.
   The Net Equity of J. Frost at January 1, 2021 was determined to be $61,000. Net Equity of J. Frost at December 31, 2021 was determined to be $67,000. Based upon the *Net Worth* method, Frost's net income for the year ended December 31, 2021 was
     A. $6,000   B. $29,500   C. $41,500   D. $55,000

Questions 5-8.

DIRECTIONS: Questions 5 through 8 are based on the following Balance Sheet, Income statement, and Notes relating to the books and records of the Hartman Corporation.

BALANCE SHEET (000 omitted)

	September 30, 2020		September 30, 2021	
	Debit	Credit	Debit	Credit
Cash	$18		$31	
Accounts Receivable	28		26	
Inventory	10		15	
Land	40		81	
Building and equipment (Net)	60		65	
Accounts Payable		$10		$11
Notes Payable		2		2
Bonds Payable		50		50
Mortgage Payable		20		46
Common Stock		50		86
Retained Earnings		24		23
	$156	$156	$218	$218

INCOME STATEMENT FOR FISCAL YEAR ENDING SEPTEMBER 30, 2021

Income:
- Sales $85
- Cost of Sales   40
- Gross Margin $45

Expenses:
- Depreciation $5
- Loss on Sale of Fixed Assets   2
- Other Operating Expenses   32
- Total Expenses $39
- Net Income $6

NOTES:
1. Dividend declared during the year 2021, $7,000
2. Acquired land; gave $36,000 common stock and cash for the balance.
3. Wrote off $1,000 accounts receivable and as uncollectible.
4. Acquired equipment; gave note secured by mortgage of $26,000.
5. Sold equipment; net cost per books, $16,000, sales price $14,000.

5. The amount of funds provided from net income for the year ended September 30 2021 is   5.____
   A. $6,000   B. $7,000   C. $13,000   D. $14,000

6. Financing and investing activities not affecting working capital are reported under the rules of APB #19. Notes 1 through 5 refer to various transactions on the books of the Hartman Corporation.   6.____
   Select the answer which refers to the numbers reflecting the concept mentioned here.
   A. Notes 1, 3, and 5   B. Notes 2 and 4
   C. Notes 2, 4, and 5   D. All five notes

7. Funds applied for the acquisition of the land are 7.____
   A. $5,000   B. $36,000   C. $41,000   D. None

8. The net change in working capital from 2020 to 2021 is 8.____
   A. $6,000   B. $16,000   C. $22,000   D. $35,000

9. Sales during July 2021 for the Magnum Corporation, operating in Los Angeles, were $378,000, of which $150,000 were on account. The sales figures given include the total sales tax charged to retail customers. (Assume a sales tax rate on all sales of 8%.) 9.____
   The CORRECT sales tax liability for July 2021 should be shown as
   A. $3,024   B. $18,240   C. $28,000   D. $30,240

10. Of the following statement ratios, the one that BEST represents a measure of cost efficiency is 10.____
    A. Acid Test Ratio
    B. Operating Costs to Net Sales Ratio
    C. Cost of Manufacturing to Plant Assets Radio
    D. Earnings Per Share

Questions 11-13.

DIRECTIONS: Questions 11 through 13 are to be answered on the basis of the following information:

An examination of the books and records of the Kay May Corporation, a machinery wholesaler, reveals the following facts for the year ended December 31, 2021:

a. Merchandise was sold and billed F.O.B. shipping point on December 31, 2021 at a sales price of $7,500. Although the merchandise costing $6,000 was ready for shipment on that date, the trucking company did not call for the merchandise until January 2, 2022. It was not included in the inventory count taken on December 31, 2021.
b. Merchandise with a sales price of $5,500 was billed and shipped to the customer on December 31, 2021. The merchandise costing $4,800 was not included in the inventory count taken on that day. Terms of sale were F.O.B. destination.
c. Merchandise costing $5,000 was recorded as a purchase on December 26, 2021. The merchandise was not included in the inventory count taken on December 31, 2021 since, upon examination, it was found to be defective and was in the process of being returned to the vendor.
d. Merchandise costing $2,500 was received on December 31, 2021. It was included in the inventory count on that date. Although the invoice was dated January 3, 2022, the purchase was recorded in the December 2021 Purchases Journal.
e. Merchandise costing $4,000 was received on January 3, 2022. It was shipped F.O.B. destination, and the invoice was dated December 30, 2021. The invoice was recorded in the December 2021 Purchases Journal, and the merchandise was included in the December 31, 2021 inventory.

11. The net change to correct the inventory value as of December 31, 2021 is: 11.____
    A. Increase $800   B. Increase $5,800
    C. Increase $6,800   D. Decrease $12,055

12. The net change to correct the sales figure for the year 2021 is: 12.____
    A. Increase $2,000   B. Decrease $5,500
    C. Decrease $7,500   D. $13,000

13. The net change to correct the purchases figure for the year 2021 is: 13.____
    A. Decrease $11,500   B. Decrease $4,000
    C. Decrease $5,000   D. Decrease $9,000

Questions 14-18.

DIRECTIONS: Each of the following Questions 14 through 18 consists of a description of a transaction that indicates a two-fold effect on the Balance Sheet. Each of these transactions may be classified under one of the following categories:

A. Assets are Understated, Retained Earnings are Understated
B. Assets are Overstated, Retained Earnings are Overstated
C. Liabilities are Understated, Retained Earnings are Overstated
D. Liabilities are Overstated, Retained Earnings are Understated

Examine each question carefully. In the correspondingly numbered space at the right, print the letter preceding the category above which BEST describes the effect of each transaction on the Balance Sheet as of December 31, 2021.

14. A major equipment purchase was made at the beginning of 2021. The equipment had an estimated six-year useful life, and depreciation was overlooked at December 31, 2021. 14.____

15. Unearned Rental Income was properly credited when received early in the year. No year-end adjustment was made to transfer the earned portion to an appropriate account. 15.____

16. Goods on hand at a branch office were excluded from the year-end physical inventory. The purchase of these goods had been properly recorded 16.____

17. Accrued Interest on Notes Receivable was overlooked as of December 31, 2021. 17.____

18. Accrued Federal Income Taxes for 2021 have never been recorded. 18.____

19. The following are account balances for the dates shown:

	Dec. 31, 2021	Dec. 31, 2020
Current Assets:		
Cash	$168,000	$60,000
Short-term investments	16,000	20,000
Accounts receivable (net)	160,000	100,000
Inventory	60,000	40,000
Prepaid expenses	4,000	40,000
Current Liabilities:		
Accounts payable	110,000	80,000
Dividends payable	30,000	0

Given the above account balances, the CHANGE in working capital is a(n)
A. increase of $128,000
B. decrease of $128,000
C. increase of $188,000
D. decrease of $188,000

20. In conducting an audit of plant assets, which of the following accounts MUST be examined in order to ascertain that additions to plant assets have been correctly stated and reflect charges that are properly capitalized?
A. Accounts receivable
B. Sales income
C. Maintenance and repairs
D. Investments

KEY (CORRECT ANSWERS)

1.	D	11.	A	
2.	D	12.	B	
3.	A	13.	D	
4.	B	14.	B	
5.	C	15.	D	
6.	B	16.	A	
7.	A	17.	A	
8.	B	18.	C	
9.	C	19.	A	
10.	B	20.	C	

EXAMINATION SECTION

TEST 1

DIRECTIONS: Each question or incomplete statement is followed by several suggested answers or completions. Select the one that BEST answers the question or completes the statement. *PRINT THE LETTER OF THE CORRECT ANSWER IN THE SPACE AT THE RIGHT.*

1. Gross income of an individual for Federal income tax purposes does NOT include
   A. interest credited to a bank savings account
   B. gain from the sale of sewer authority bonds
   C. back pay received as a result of job reinstatement
   D. interest received from State Dormitory Authority bonds

   1.____

2. A cash-basis, calendar-year taxpayer purchased an annuity policy at a total cost of $20,000. Starting on January 1 of 2022, he began to receive annual payments of $1,500. His life expectancy as of that date was 16 years. The amount of annuity income to be included in his gross income for the taxable year 2022 is
   A. none   B. $250   C. $1,250   D. $1,500

   2.____

3. The transactions related to a municipal police retirement system should be included in a(n) _____ fund.
   A. intra-governmental service   B. trust
   C. general   D. special revenue

   3.____

4. The budget for a given cost during a given period was $100,000. The actual cost for the period was $90,000.
   Based upon these facts, one should say that the responsible manager has done a better than expected job in controlling the cost if the cost is _____ budgeted production.
   A. variable and actual production equaled
   B. a discretionary fixed cost and actual production equaled
   C. variable and actual production was 90% of
   D. variable and actual production was 80% of

   4.____

5. In the conduct of an audit, the MOST practical method by which an accountant can satisfy himself as to the physical existence of inventory is to
   A. be present and observe personally the audited firm's physical inventory being taken
   B. independently verify an adequate proportion of all inventory operations performed by the audited firm
   C. mail confirmation requests to vendors of merchandise sold to the audited firm within the inventory year
   D. review beforehand the adequacy of the audited firm's plan for inventory taking, and during the actual inventory-taking states, verify that this plan is being followed

   5.____

Questions 6-7.

DIRECTIONS: Questions 6 and 7 are to be answered on the basis of the following information.

For the month of March, the ABC Manufacturing Corporation's estimated factory overhead for an expected volume of 15,000 lbs. of a product was as follows:

	Amount	Overhead Rate Per Unit
Fixed Overhead	$3,000	$.20
Variable Overhead	$9,000	$.60

Actual volume was 10,000 lbs. and actual overhead expense was $7,700.

6. The Spending (Budget) Variance was _____ (Favorable).
   A. $1,300   B. $6,000   C. $7,700   D. $9,000

7. The Idle Capacity Variance was
   A. $300 (Favorable)
   B. $1,000 (Unfavorable)
   C. $1,300 (Favorable)
   D. $8,000 (Unfavorable)

Questions 8-11.

DIRECTIONS: Questions 8 through 11 are to be answered on the basis of the following information.

A bookkeeper, who was not familiar with proper accounting procedures, prepared the following financial report for Largor Corporation as of December 31, 2021. In addition to the errors in presentation, additional data below was not considered in the preparation of the report. Restate this balance sheet in proper form, giving recognition to the additional data, so that you will be able to determine the required information to answer Questions 8 through 11.

LARGOR CORPORATION
December 31, 2021

Current Assets			
Cash		$110,000	
Marketable Securities		53,000	
Accounts Receivable	$261,400		
Accounts Payable	125,000	136,400	
Inventories		274,000	
Prepaid Expenses		24,000	
Treasury Stock		20,000	
Cash Surrender Value of Officers' Life Insurance Policies		105,000	$722,400
Plant Assets			
Equipment		350,000	
Building	200,000		
Reserve for Plant Expansion	75,000	125,000	
Land		47,500	
TOTAL ASSETS			$1,244,900

3 (#1)

Liabilities
Salaries Payable 16,500
Cash Dividend Payable 50,000
Stock Dividend Payable 70,000
Bonds Payable 200,000
  Less Sinking Fund 90,000   110,000
TOTAL LIABILITIES $246,500

Stockholders' Equity:
  Paid In Capital
    Common Stock   350,000

Retained Earnings and Reserves
  Reserve for Income Taxes   90,000
  Reserve for Doubtful Accounts   6,500
  Reserve for Treasury Stock   20,000
  Reserve for Depreciation Equipment   70,000
  Reserve for Depreciation Building   80,000
  Premium on Common Stock   15,000
  Retained Earnings   366,900   648,400   998,400

TOTAL LIABILITIES & EQUITY   1,244,900

Additional Data
  A. Bond Payable will mature eight (8) years from Balance Sheet date.
  B. The Stock Dividend Payable was declared on December 31, 2021.
  C. The Reserve for Income Taxes represents the balance due on the estimated liability for taxes on income for the year ended December 31.
  D. Advances from Customers at the Balance Sheet date totaled $13,600. This total is still credited against Accounts Receivable.
  E. Prepaid Expenses include Unamortized Mortgage Costs of $15,000.
  F. Marketable Securities were recorded at cost. Their market value at December 31, 2021 was $50,800.

8. After restatement of the balance sheet in proper form and giving recognition to the additional data, the Total Current Assets should be   8._____
   A. $597,400   B. $702,400   C. $712,300   D. $827,300

9. After restatement of the balance sheet in proper form and giving recognition to the additional data, the Total Current Liabilities should be   9._____
   A. $261,500   B. $281,500   C. $295,100   D. $370,100

10. After restatement of the balance sheet in proper form and giving recognition to the additional data, the net book value of plant and equipment should be   10._____
   A. $400,000   B. $447,500   C. $550,000   D. $597,500

11. After restatement of the balance sheet in proper form and giving recognition to the additional data, the Stockholders Equity should be   11._____
   A. $320,000   B. $335,000   C. $764,700   D. $874,700

4 (#1)

12. When preparing the financial statement, dividends in arrears on preferred stock should be treated as a
    A. contingent liability
    B. deduction from capital
    C. parenthetical remark
    D. valuation reserve

    12._____

13. The IPC Corporation has an intangible asset which it values at $1,000,000 and has a life expectancy of 60 years.
    The appropriate span of write-off, as determined by good accounting practice, should be _____ years.
    A. 17   B. 34   C. 40   D. 60

    13._____

14. The following information was used in costing inventory on October 31:
    October 1 - Beginning inventory   800 units   @ $1.20
             4 - Received   200 units   @ $1.40
            16 - Issued   400 units
            24 - Received   200 units   @ $1.60
            27 - Issued   500 units

    Using the LIFO method of inventory evaluation (end-of-month method), the total dollar value of the inventory at October 31 was
    A. $360   B. $460   C. $600   D. $1,200

    14._____

15. If a $400,000 par value bond issue paying 8%, with interest dates of June 30 and December 31, is sold in November 1 for par plus accrued interest, the cash proceeds received by the issuer on November 1 should be APPROXIMATELY
    A. $405,000   B. $408,000   C. $411,000   D. $416,000

    15._____

16. The TOTAL interest cost to the issuer of a bond issue sold for more than its face value is the periodic interest payment _____ amortization.
    A. plus the discount
    B. plus the premium
    C. minus the discount
    D. minus the premium

    16._____

17. If shareholders donate shares of stock back to the company, such stock received by the company is properly classified as
    A. Treasury stock
    B. Unissued stock
    C. Other assets – investment
    D. Current assets - investment

    17._____

18. Assume the following transactions have occurred:
    1. 10,000 shares of capital stock of Omer Corp., par value $50, have been sold and issued on initial sale @ $55 per share during the month of June
    2. 2,000 shares of previously issued stock were purchased from shareholders during the month of September @ $58 per share.

    As of September 30, the stockholders' equity section TOTAL should be
    A. $434,000   B. $450,000   C. $480,000   D. $550,000

    18._____

19. Mr. Diak, a calendar-year taxpayer in the construction business, agrees to construct a building for the Supermat Corporation to cost a total of $500,000 and to require about two years to complete. By December 31, 2021, he has expended $150,000 in costs, and it was determined that the building was 35% completed.
    If Mr. Diak is reporting income under the completed contract method, the amount of gross income he will report for 2021 is
    A. none   B. $25,000   C. $175,000   D. $350,000

20. When the Board of Directors of a firm uses the present-value technique to aid in deciding whether or not to buy a new plant asset, it needs to have information reflecting
    A. the cost of the new asset only
    B. the increased production from use of new asset only
    C. an estimated rate of return
    D. the book value of the asset

KEY (CORRECT ANSWERS)

1.	D	11.	D
2.	B	12.	C
3.	B	13.	C
4.	A	14.	A
5.	D	15.	C
6.	A	16.	D
7.	B	17.	A
8.	C	18.	A
9.	C	19.	A
10.	B	20.	C

TEST 2

DIRECTIONS: Each question or incomplete statement is followed by several suggested answers or completions. Select the one that BEST answers the question or completes the statement. *PRINT THE LETTER OF THE CORRECT ANSWER IN THE SPACE AT THE RIGHT.*

Questions 1-3.

DIRECTIONS: Questions 1 through 3 are to be answered on the basis of the following information.

During your audit of the Avon Company, you find the following errors in the records of the company:

1. Incorrect exclusion from the final inventory of items costing $3,000 for which the purchase was not recorded.
2. Inclusion in the final inventory of goods costing $5,000, although a purchase was not recorded. The goods in question were being held on consignment from Reldrey Company.
3. Incorrect exclusion of $2,000 from the inventory count at the end of the period. The goods were in transit (F.O.B. shipping point); the invoice had been received and the purchase recorded.
4. Inclusion of items on the receiving dock that were being held for return to the vendor because of damage. In counting the goods in the receiving department, these items were incorrectly included. With respect to these goods, a purchase of $4,000 had been recorded.

The records (uncorrected) showed the following amounts:
1. Purchases, $170,000
2. Pretax income, $15,000
3. Accounts payable, $20,000; and
4. Inventory at the end of the period, $40,000.

1. The CORRECTED inventory is
   A. $36,000   B. $42,000   C. $43,000   D. $44,000

2. The CORRECTED income for the year is
   A. $12,000   B. $15,000   C. $17,000   D. $18,000

3. The CORRECT accounts payable liabilities are
   A. $16,000   B. $17,000   C. $19,000   D. $23,000

4. An auditing procedure that is MOST likely to reveal the existence of a contingent liability is
   A. a review of vouchers paid during the month following the year end
   B. confirmation of accounts payable
   C. an inquiry directed to legal counsel
   D. confirmation of mortgage notes

2 (#2)

Questions 5-6.

DIRECTIONS: Questions 5 and 6 are to be answered on the basis of the following information.

Mr. Zelev operates a business as a sole proprietor and uses the cash basis for reporting income for income tax purposes. His bank account during 2021 for the business shows receipts totaling $285,000 and cash payments totaling $240,000. Included in the cash payments were payments for three-year business insurance policies whose premiums totaled $1,575. It was determined that the expired premiums for this year were $475. Further examination of the accounts and discussion with Mr. Zelev revealed the fact that included in the receipts were the following items, as well as the proceeds received from customers:

$15,000 which Mr. Zelev took from his savings account and deposited in the business account.
$20,000 which Mr. Zelev received from the bank as a loan which will be repaid next year.
Included in the cash payments were $10,000, which Mr. Zelev took on a weekly basis from the business receipts to use for his personal expenses.

5. The amount of net income to be reported for income tax purposes for calendar year 2022 for Mr. Zelev is
    A. $21,100   B. $26,100   C. $31,100   D. $46,100

5._____

6. Assuming the same facts as those reported above, Mr. Zelev would be required to pay a self-employment tax for 2022 of
    $895.05   B. $1,208.70   C. $1,234.35   D. $1,666.90

6._____

7. For the year ended December 2021, you are given the following information relative to the income and expense statements for the Sungam Manufacturers, Inc.:
    Sales.. $1,000.000
    Sales Returns.. 95,000

7._____

Cost of Sales
Opening Inventories $200,000
Purchases During the Year   567,000
Direct Labor Costs   240,000
Factory Overhead   24,400
Inventories End of Year   235,000

On June 5, 2021, a fire destroyed the plant and all of the inventories then on hand. You are given the following information and asked to ascertain the amount of the estimated inventory loss.

Sales up to June 15 $545,000
Purchased to June 15   254,500
Direct Labor   233,000
Overhead   14,550
Salvaged Inventory   95,000

The ESTIMATED inventory loss is
A. $96,000   B. $162,450   C. $189,450   D. $257,450

8. Losses and excessive costs with regard to inventory can occur in any one of several operating functions of an organization.
The operating function which bears the GREATEST responsibility for the failure to give proper consideration to transportation costs of material acquisitions is
A. accounting   B. purchasing   C. receiving   D. shipping

Questions 9-17.

DIRECTIONS: Questions 9 through 17 are to be answered on the basis of the following information.

You are conducting an audit of the PAP Company, which has a contract to supply the municipal hospitals with specialty refrigerators on a cost-plus basis. The following information is available:

Materials Purchased	$1,946,700
Inventories, January 1	
Materials	268,000
Finished Goods (100 units)	43,000
Direct Labor	2,125,800
Factory Overhead (40% variable)	764,000
Marketing Expenses (all fixed)	516,000
Administrative Expenses (all fixed)	461,000
Sales (12,400 units)	6,634,000
Inventories, March 31	
Materials	167,000
Finished Goods (200 units)	(omitted)
No Work in Process	

9. The NET INCOME for the period is
A. $755,500   B. $1,237,500   C. $1,732,500   D. $4,980,500

10. The number of units manufactured is
A. 12,400   B. 12,500   C. 12,600   D. 12,700

11. The unit cost of refrigerators manufactured is MOST NEARLY
A. $389.00   B. $395.00   C. $398.00   D. $400.00

12. The TOTAL variable costs are
A. $305,600   B. $464,000   C. $4,479,100   D. $4,937,500

13. The TOTAL fixed costs are
A. $458,400   B. $1,435,400   C. $1,471,800   D. $1,741,000

While you are conducting your audit, the PAP Company advises you that they have changed their inventory costing from FIFO to LIFO. You are interested in pursuing the matter further because this change will affect the cost of the refrigerators. An examination of material part 2-317 inventory card shows the following activity:

May 2 – Received 100 units @ $5.40 per unit
May 8 – Received 30 units @ $8.00 per unit
May 15 – Issued 50 units
May 22 – Received 120 units @ $9.00 per unit
May 29 – Issued 100 units

14. Using the FIFO method under a perpetual inventory control system, the TOTAL cost of the units issued in May is
 A. $690   B. $960   C. $1,590   D. $1,860

15. Using the FIFO method under a perpetual inventory control system, the VALUE of the closing inventory is
 A. $780   B. $900   C. $1,080   D. $1,590

16. Using the LIFO method under a perpetual inventory control system, the TOTAL cost of the units issued in May is
 A. $1,248   B. $1,428   C. $1,720   D. $1,860

17. Using the LIFO method under a perpetual inventory control system, the value of the closing inventory is
 A. $612   B. $380   C. $1,512   D. $1,680

Questions 18-20.

DIRECTIONS: For Questions 18 through 20, consider that the EEF Corporation has a fully integrated cost accounting system.

18. Unit cost of manufacturing dresses was $7.00. Spoiled dresses numbered 400 with a sales value of $800.
 When it is not customary to have a Spoiled Work account, the MOST appropriate account to be credited is
 A. Work in Process   B. Cost of Sales
 C. Manufacturing Overhead   D. Finished Goods

19. Overtime premium for factory workers (direct labor) totaled $400 for the payroll period. This was due to inadequate plant capacity.
 The account to be DEBITED is
 A. Work in Process   B. Cost of Sales
 C. Manufacturing Overhead   D. Finished Goods

20. A month-end physical inventory of stores shows a shortage of $175. The account to be DEBITED to correct this shortage is
    A. Stores
    B. Work in Process
    C. Cost of Sales
    D. Manufacturing Overhead

20.____

KEY (CORRECT ANSWERS)

1. A
2. A
3. C
4. C
5. A

6. D
7. B
8. B
9. A
10. B

11. B
12. C
13. B
14. B
15. B

16. A
17. A
18. A
19. C
20. C

ACCOUNTING

EXAMINATION SECTION
TEST 1

DIRECTIONS: Each question or incomplete statement is followed by several suggested answers or completions. Select the one that BEST answers the question or completes the statement. PRINT THE LETTER OF THE CORRECT ANSWER IN THE SPACE AT THE RIGHT.

Questions 1-5.

DIRECTIONS: Assume that you are requested to verify certain financial data with respect to the various business entities described below. This information is required to verify that tax returns and/or other financial reports submitted to your agency are correct.

In an auditing review of the income statements of several business firms (Companies X, Y, and Z), you find the financial information given below. Based upon the account balances shown, select the correct answer for the statement information requested.

Company X - Sales $ 160,000
             Opening Inventory $ 70,000
             Purchases $ 80,000
             Purchase Returns $ 1,200
             Cost of Goods Sold $ 127,000

1. The ending inventory based upon the data above is

   A. $21,800   B. $23,000   C. $24,200   D. $33,000

   Company Y - Opening Inventory $ 50,000
                Purchases $ 145,000
                Ending Inventory $ 28,500
                Gross Profit $ 56,000
                Sales and Administrative Expenses $ 64,000

2. Sales for the period based upon the data above are

   A. $110,500   B. $166,500   C. $222,500   D. $286,500

   Company Z - Sales for the period $ 200,000
                Net Profit   7% of Sales
                Purchases $ 180,000
                Ending Inventory $ 70,000
                Gross Profit $ 60,000

3. Cost of Goods sold for Company Z is

   A. $110,000   B. $140,000   C. $180,000   D. $250,000

4. The opening inventory of Company Z would be

   A. $10,000   B. $20,000   C. $30,000   D. $80,000

5. The operating expenses for Company Z would be

   A. $10,000   B. $14,000   C. $20,000   D. $46,000

Questions 6-8.

DIRECTIONS: The following information is taken from the books and records of a business firm:

Sales for the calendar year 2018:	$52,000
Based upon FIFO Inventory:	
Good available for Sale	$46,900
Inventory at December 31, 2018	$12,700
Based upon LIFO Inventory:	
Goods available for Sale	$46,900
Inventory at December 31, 2018	$10,400

6. If FIFO Inventory valuation is used, the Gross Profit will be

   A. $5,100   B. $15,500   C. $17,800   D. $34,200

7. If LIFO Inventory valuation method is used, the Gross Profit will be

   A. $2,300   B. $15,500   C. $17,800   D. $36,500

8. If LIFO Inventory method is used, compared with the FIFO method, the cost of goods sold will be

   A. more by $2,300   B. less by $2,300
   C. more by $10,400   D. less by $12,700

9. Which one of the following would NOT properly be classified as an asset on the balance sheet of a business firm?

   A. Investment in stock of another firm
   B. Premium cost of a three-year fire insurance policy
   C. Cash surrender value of life insurance on life of corporate officer. Policy is owned by the company and the company is the beneficiary
   D. Amounts owing to employees for services rendered

10. Which one of the following would NOT properly be classified as a current asset?

    A. Travel advances to salespeople
    B. Postage in a postage meter
    C. Cash surrender value of life insurance policy on an officer, which policy names the corporation as the beneficiary
    D. Installment notes receivable due over 18 months in accordance with normal trade practice

11. Able, Baker and Carr formed a partnership. Able contributed $10,000, Baker contributed $5,000, and Carr contributed an automobile with a fair market value of $5,000. They have no partnership agreement. The first year the partnership earned $18,000.
    The partners will share the profits as follows:

    A. Able, $9,000; Baker, $4,500; Carr, $4,500
    B. Able, $6,000; Baker, $6,000; Carr, $6,000
    C. Able, $12,000; Baker, $6,000; Carr, No share
    D. Able, $8,000; Baker, $5,000; Carr, $5,000

Questions 12-13.

DIRECTIONS: Answer Questions 12 through 13 based on the information below.

The XYZ partnership had the following balance sheet as of December 31, 2018.
Cash	$ 5,000	Liabilities	$ 12,000
Other assets	40,000	X Capital	20,000
Total	$45,000	Y Capital	10,000
		Z Capital	3,000
		Total	$45,000

The partners shared profits equally. They decided to liquidate the partnership at December 31, 2018.

12. If the other assets were sold for $52,000, each partner will be entitled to a final cash distribution of

   A. X, $15,000; Y, $15,000; Z, $15,000
   B. X, $24,000; Y, $14,000; Z, $ 7,000
   C. X, $20,000; Y, $10,000; Z, $ 3,000
   D. X, $23,000; Y, $13,000; Z, $ 6,000

13. If the other assets were sold for $31,000, each partner will be entitled to a final cash distribution of

   A. X, $14,000; Y, $ 5,000; Z, $5,000
   B. X, $ 8,000; Y, R 8,000; Z, $8,000
   C. X, $15,000; Y, $15,000; Z, $15,000
   D. X, $17,000; Y, $ 7,000; Z, No cash share

14. Items selling for $40 for which there were 10% selling costs were purchased for inventory at $20 each. Selling prices and costs remained steady but at the date of the financial statement the market price had dropped to $16. The inventory remaining from the original purchase was written down to $16.
Of the following, it is correct to state that the

   A. cost of sales of the subsequent year will be overstated
   B. current year's income is overstated
   C. income of the following year will be overstated
   D. closing inventory of the current year is overstated

15. Dividends in arrears on a cumulative preferred stock should be reported on the balance sheet as

   A. an accrued liability
   B. restricted retained earnings
   C. an explanatory note
   D. a deduction from preferred stock

16. The effect of recording the payment of a 10% dividend paid in stock would be to

   A. *increase* the current ratio
   B. *decrease* the amount of working capital
   C. *increase* the total stockholder equity
   D. *decrease* the book value per share of stock outstanding

17. The owner of a truck which originally had cost $12,000 but now has a book value of $1,500 was offered $3,000 for it by a used truck dealer. However, the owner traded it in for a new truck listed at $19,000 and received a trade-in allowance of $4,000.
    The cost basis for the new truck, following the Federal income tax rules, *properly* amounts to

    A. $15,000   B. $16,000   C. $16,500   D. $17,500

18. In planning for purchases to be made during the next month, the following information is to be used:
    Budgeted sales for the month   73,000 units
    Inventory at beginning of the month   19,000 units
    Planned inventory at end of the month   14,000 units
    From the above information, the number of units to be purchased is

    A. 40,000   B. 59,000   C. 68,000   D. 78,000

19. A branch office of a company has the following plan:
    Cash balance at beginning of the month $ 10,000
    Planned cash balance at end of the month $ 15,000
    Expected receipts for the month $ 180,000
    Expected disbursements for the month $ 205,000
    In order to comply with this plan, the accountant should recommend that the branch obtain an additional allocation of

    A. $20,000   B. $25,000   C. $30,000   D. $50,000

20. A company uses the reserve method of bad debt expense and sets up a Bad Debt account at 2% of sales. The sales were $500,000. The company wrote off $7,500 in accounts receivable.
    The effect of these entries on net income for the period is a(n)

    A. $2,500 increase   B. $7,500 decrease
    C. $8,000 decrease   D. $10,000 decrease

KEY (CORRECT ANSWERS)

1.	A	11.	B
2.	C	12.	B
3.	B	13.	D
4.	C	14.	C
5.	D	15.	C
6.	C	16.	D
7.	B	17.	C
8.	A	18.	C
9.	D	19.	C
10.	C	20.	D

TEST 2

DIRECTIONS: Each question or incomplete statement is followed by several suggested answers or completions. Select the one that *BEST* answers the question or completes the statement. *PRINT THE LETTER OF THE CORRECT ANSWER IN THE SPACE AT THE RIGHT.*

1. The Delox Corporation has applied to their bank for a $50,000 loan which they will need for 90 days. The bank grants the loan, which will be discounted at 7% interest. The Delox Corporation will receive credit in their account at the bank for (based on a 360-day year):

   A. $46,500   B. $49,125   C. $50,000   D. $50,875

   1.____

Questions 2-5.

DIRECTIONS: Answer Questions 2 through 5 based on the information below.

Assume that you are reviewing some accounts of a company and find the following: The Machinery Account and the Accumulated Depreciation - Machinery Account.

```
                              MACHINERY
Jan. 1, 2015    Machine #1    20,000   |   July 1, 2016    6,000
Jan. 1, 2016    Machine #2    16,000   |
July 1, 2016    Machine #3    12,000   |
Jan. 1, 2018    Machine #4    20,000   |

              ACCUMULATED DEPRECIATION - MACHINERY
                                       |   Dec. 31, 2015    5,000
                                       |   Dec. 31, 2016   10,500
```

Machines are depreciated based upon a four-year life and using the straight-line method. Assume no salvage values.

On July 1, 2016, Machine #1, purchased on January 1, 2015, was sold for $6,000 cash. The bookkeeper debited Cash and credited Machinery for $6,000.

On January 1, 2018, Machine #2 was traded in for a newer model. The new Machine had a list price of $34,000. A trade-in value of $10,000 was granted. $20,000 was paid in cash and the bookkeeper debited Machinery and credited Cash for $20,000. Income-tax rules should have been applied making this entry.

If any errors were made in recording the machine values or depreciation, you are asked to correct them and determine the corrected asset values and proper accumulated depreciation.

2. As of December 31, 2015, you determine that these two accounts

   A. are correct
   B. are incorrect
   C. overstate asset book values
   D. understate asset book values

   2.____

3. As of December 31, 2016, you determine that, to correct the Machinery Account Balance, you should leave it

   A. unchanged   B. increased by $6,000
   C. decreased by $14,000   D. decreased by $5,500

   3.____

25

4. As of December 31, 2016, you determine that, to reflect the proper balance, the Accumulated Depreciation - Machinery account should

   A. remain unchanged
   B. be increased by $10,000
   C. be decreased by $10,000
   D. be decreased by $ 5,500

5. After the January 1, 2018 entry, you determine that the Machinery Account should, *properly*,

   A. remain unchanged
   B. reflect a corrected balance of $52,000
   C. reflect a corrected balance of $40,000
   D. reflect a corrected balance of $56,000

Questions 6-9.

DIRECTIONS: Answer Questions 6 through 9 based on the information below.

Assume that you are assigned to prepare an Audit Report Summary on the L Company. The L Company uses the accrual method and has an accounting year ending December 31. The bookkeeper of the company has made the following errors:
1. A $1,500 collection from a customer was received on December 29, 2017, but not recorded until the date of its deposit in the bank, January 4, 2018
2. A supplier's $1,900 invoice for inventory items received December 2017 was not recorded until January 2018 (Inventories at December 31, 2017 and 2018 were stated correctly, based on physical count)
3. Depreciation for 2017 was understated by $700
4. In September 2017, a $350 invoice for office supplies was charged to the Utilities Expense account. Office supplies are expensed as purchased
5. December 31, 2017, sales on account of $2,500 were recorded in January 2018, although the merchandise had been shipped and was not in the inventory

Assume that no other errors have occurred and that no correcting entries have been made. Ignore all income taxes.

6. After correcting the errors reported above, the corrected Net Income for 2017 was

   A. overstated by $100
   B. understated by $800
   C. understated by $1,800
   D. neither understated nor overstated

7. Working Capital on December 31, 2017 was

   A. understated by $600
   B. understated by $2,300
   C. understated by $1,200
   D. neither understated nor overstated

8. Total Assets on December 31, 2018 were

   A. overstated by $1,100
   B. overstated by $1,800

C. understated by $850
D. neither understated nor overstated

9. The cash balance was

   A. correct as stated originally
   B. overstated by $1,500
   C. understated by $2,500
   D. understated by $1,500

Questions 10-13.

DIRECTIONS: Answer Questions 10 through 13 based on the information below.

Salary expense was listed as a total of $27,600 for the month of June 2018. Withholding taxes were determined to be $7,250 for Income taxes and $1,170 for FICA taxes withheld from employees. Payroll deductions for employee pension fund contribution amounted to $2,500.
Assume the employer's FICA tax share is equal to the employees' and that the employer's share of pension costs is double that of the employees and the employer also pays a 3% Unemployment Insurance Tax based upon $20,000 of the wages paid. The employer pays $1,500 for health insurance plans.

10. The amount of cash that must be obtained to meet this net payroll to pay employees is

    A. $16,680   B. $19,180   C. $20,350   D. $27,600

11. The total payroll tax expense for this payroll period is

    A. $1,170   B. $1,760   C. $2,340   D. $2,940

12. The total liability for withholding and payroll taxes payable is

    A. $2,340   B. $7,250   C. $8,420   D. $10,190

13. The expense of the employer for pension and health-care fringe benefits is

    A. $1,500   B. $2,500   C. $5,000   D. $6,500

14. Currently preferred terminology for statements to be presented limits the use of the term "reserve" to

    A. an actual liability of a known amount
    B. estimated liabilities
    C. appropriations of retained earnings
    D. valuation (contra) accounts

Questions 15-16.

DIRECTIONS: Answer Questions 15 through 16 based on the following.

The Victory Corporation provides an incentive plan whereby its president receives a bonus equal to 10% of the corporate income in excess of $150,000. The bonus is based upon income before income taxes but after calculating the bonus.

15. If the income for the calendar year 2018, before income taxes and before the bonus were $480,000 and the effective tax rate is 40%, the amount of the bonus would be

A. $15,000   B. $30,000   C. $33,000   D. $48,000

16. The income tax expense for calendar year 2012 would be 16.___

A. $60,000   B. $132,000   C. $180,000   D. $192,000

Questions 17-18.

DIRECTIONS: Answer Questions 17 through 18 based on the information below.

A contract has been awarded to the low bidder. This contractor will then commence construction of a building for the total contract price of $30,000,000. The expected cost of construction is $27,510,000. You are given the additional facts:

	2016	2017	2018
Contract Price as above	$ 30,000,000	$ 30,000,000	$ 30,000,000
Actual Cost to date	$ 9,170,000	$ 13,755,000	$ 27,510,000
Estimated Cost to complete	18,340,000	13,755,000	
Estimated Total Cost	$ 27,510,000	$ 27,510,000	$ 27,510,000
Estimated Total Income	$ 2,490,000	$	$
Billings	$ 9,000,000	$ 9,000,000	$ 9,000,000

17. For 2016, the income to be recognized on a percentage-of-completion basis would be 17.___

A. $830,000   B. $2,490,000
C. $3,000,000   D. $9,000,000

18. For 2017, the income to be recognized by the contractor on a percentage-of-completion basis would be 18.___

A. $415,000   B. $424,500   C. $830,000   D. $1,245,000

19. If the city borrows the $9,000,000 to pay the first billing for the contract above at 10% interest for two years, and the second $9,000,000 at 7% interest for one year, then the interest costs related to this building are, approximately, 19.___

A. $630,000   B. $1,800,000
C. $2,430,000   D. $3,000,000

20. The books of the Monmouth Corporation show the following: 20.___

	2018	2017	2016
Average earnings for prior 3 years	$70,000	$75,000	$78,000
Net tangible assets	$40,000	$42,000	$50,000

If it is expected that 15% would be normal earnings on net tangible assets, then the *average* excess earnings are

A. $7,120   B. $8,333   C. $9,800   D. $10,800

21. A business showed the following figures in its accounts for the year 2018: 21.___
   Sales - $346,000
   Inventory, December 31, 2018 - $58,000
   Inventory, December 31, 2017 - $52,000
   Purchases - $274,000
   Operating Expenses - $36,000
The gross profit earned by this concern is

A. $72,000   B. $42,000   C. $66,000   D. $78,000

22. A business firm buys an article for $320, less 40% and 10%, terms 2/10 n/30, on March 18. If it pays the bill on March 27, it should pay

   A. $169.34   B. $172.80   C. $160.00   D. $156.80

23. In the partnership of Danvers and Edwards, Danvers has a capital of $10,000 and Edwards has a capital of $15,000. If Furgal wishes to invest $11,000 and thereby receive a 1/4 interest in the business, the goodwill in the business has been computed to be worth

   A. $19,000   B. $33,000   C. $14,000   D. $8,000

24. George Bailey's capital at the beginning of the year was $14,000. At the end of the year his assets were $62,000 and his liabilities were $39,000. His drawings for the year amounted to $6,000.
   His profit for the year was

   A. $15,000   B. $3,000   C. $9,000   D. $17,000

25. George Wilson's check book shows the following:

   Balance at the beginning of the month   -$3,517.42
   Deposits during the month   -$1,923.98
   Checks drawn during the month   -$2,144.36

   In going over his bank statement, he finds that a deposit of $455.64 made by him has not yet been credited by the bank and that the bank has charged him $9.40 for services rendered. He also finds that he has outstanding checks totaling $268.19.
   His bank statement balance should be printed as

   A. $3,100.19   B. $3,118.99   C. $2,563.81   D. $4,011.47

KEY (CORRECT ANSWERS)

1. B		11. B	
2. A		12. D	
3. C		13. D	
4. C		14. C	
5. C		15. B	
6. A		16. C	
7. A		17. A	
8. B		18. A	
9. D		19. C	
10. A		20. B	

21. D
22. A
23. D
24. A
25. A

EXAMINATION SECTION

DIRECTIONS: Each question or incomplete statement is followed by several suggested answers or completions. Select the one that BEST answers the question or completes the statement. *PRINT THE LETTER OF THE CORRECT ANSWER IN THE SPACE AT THE RIGHT.*

1. When a principal auditor decides to make reference to another auditor's examination, the principal auditor's report should always indicate clearly, in the introductory, scope, and opinion paragraphs, the
    A. magnitude of the portion of the financial statements examined by the other auditor
    B. disclaimer of responsibility concerning the portion of the financial statements examined by the other auditor
    C. name of the other auditor
    D. division of responsibility

2. When there is a significant change in accounting principle, an auditor's report should refer to the lack of consistency in
    A. the scope paragraph
    B. an explanatory paragraph between the second paragraph and the opinion paragraph
    C. the opinion paragraph
    D. an explanatory paragraph following the opinion paragraph

3. How are management's responsibility and the auditor's responsibility represented in the standard author's report?

	Management's responsibility	Auditor's responsibility
A.	Explicitly	Explicitly
B.	Implicity	Implicitly
C.	Implicity	Explicitly
D.	Explicity	Implicitly

4. Restrictions imposed by a client prohibit the observation of physical inventories, which account for 35% of all assets. Alternative audit procedures cannot be applied, although the auditor was able to examine satisfactory evidence for all other items in the financial statements. The auditor should issue a(n)
    A. "except for" qualified opinion
    B. disclaimer of opinion
    C. unqualified opinion with a separate explanatory paragraph
    D. unqualified opinion with an explanation in the scope paragraph

5. When an accountant performs more than one level of service (for example, a compilation and a review, or a compilation and an audit) concerning the financial statements of a nonpublic entity, the accountant generally should issue the report that is appropriate for
   A. the lowest level of service rendered
   B. the highest level of service rendered
   C. a compilation engagement
   D. a review engagement

5.____

6. An accountant who reviews the financial statements of a nonpublic entity should issue a report stating that a review
   A. is substantially less in scope than an audit
   B. provides negative assurance that the internal control structure is functioning as designed
   C. provides only limited assurance that the financial statements are fairly presented
   D. is substantially more in scope than a compilation

6.____

7. A limitation on the scope of an auditor's examination sufficient to preclude an unqualified opinion will usually result when management
   A. presents financial statements that are prepared in accordance with the cash receipts and disbursements basis of accounting
   B. states that the financial statements are not intended to be presented in conformity with generally accepted accounting principles
   C. does not make the minutes of the Board of Directors' meetings available to the auditor
   D. asks the auditor to report on the balance sheet and not on the other basic financial statements

7.____

8. Grant Company's financial statements adequately disclose uncertainties that concern future events, the outcome of which are not susceptible of reasonable estimation. The auditor's report should include a(n) _____ opinion.
   A. unqualified
   B. "subject to" qualified
   C. "except for" qualified
   D. adverse

8.____

9. An auditor concludes that there is substantial doubt about an entity's ability to continue as a going concern for a reasonable period of time. If the entity's disclosures concerning this matter are adequate, the audit report may include a(n)

	Disclaimer of opinion	"Except for" qualified opinion
A.	Yes	Yes
B.	No	No
C.	No	Yes
D.	Yes	No

9.____

10. An auditor may issue a qualified opinion under which of the following circumstances?

	Lack of sufficient competent evidential matter	Restrictions on the scope of the audit
A.	Yes	Yes
B.	Yes	No
C.	No	Yes
D.	No	No

11. When reporting on comparative financial statements, an auditor ordinarily should change the previously issued opinion on the prior year's financial statements if
    A. the prior year's opinion was unqualified and the opinion on the current year's financial statements is modified due to a lack of consistency
    B. the prior year's financial statements are restated following a pooling of interests in the current year
    C. the prior year's financial statements are restated to conform with generally accepted accounting principles
    D. the auditor is a predecessor auditor who has been requested by a former client to reissue the previously issued report

12. Does an auditor make the following representations explicity or implicitly when issuing the standard auditor's report on comparative financial statements?

	Consistent application of accounting principles	Examination of evidence on a test basis
A.	Explicitly	Explicitly
B.	Implicitly	Implicitly
C.	Implicitly	Explicity
D.	Explicitly	Implicitly

13. An auditor should disclose the substantive reasons for expressing an adverse opinion in an explanatory paragraph
    A. preceding the scope paragraph
    B. preceding the opinion paragraph
    C. following the opinion paragraph
    D. within the notes to the financial statements

14. When management does not provide reasonable justification that a change in accounting principle is preferable and it presents comparative financial statements, the auditor should express a qualified opinion
    A. only in the year of the accounting principle change
    B. each year that the financial statements initially reflecting the change are presented
    C. each year until management changes back to the accounting principle formerly used
    D. only if the change is to an accounting principle that is not generally accepted

15. When an accountant compiles a nonpublic entity's financial statements that omit substantially all disclosures required by generally accepted accounting principles, the accountant should indicate in the compilation report that the financial statements are
    A. restricted for internal use only by the entity's management
    B. not to be given to financial institutions for the purpose of obtaining credit
    C. compiled in conformity with a comprehensive basis of accounting other than generally accepted accounting principles
    D. not designed for those who are uninformed about the omitted disclosures

16. When an independent CPA is associated with the financial statements of a publicly held entity but has not audited or reviewed such statements, the appropriate form of report to be issued must include a(n)
    A. compilation report
    B. disclaimer of opinion
    C. unaudited association report
    D. qualified opinion

17. The objective of a review of interim financial information is to provide an accountant with a basis for reporting whether
    A. the financial statements are presented fairly in accordance with generally accepted accounting principles
    B. a reasonable basis exists for expressing an updated opinion regarding the financial statements that were previously audited
    C. material modifications should be made to conform with generally accepted accounting principles
    D. the financial statements are presented fairly in accordance with standards of interim reporting

18. When an auditor is requested to express an opinion on the rental and royalty income of an entity, the auditor may
    A. not accept the engagement because to do so would be tantamount to agreeing to issue a piecemeal opinion
    B. not accept the engagement unless also engaged to audit the full financial statements of the entity
    C. accept the engagement provided the auditor's opinion is expressed in a special report
    D. accept the engagement provided distribution of the auditor's report is limited to the entity's management

19. Negative assurance may be expressed when an accountant is requested to report on the
    A. compilation of prospective financial statements
    B. compliance with the provisions of the Foreign Corrupt Practices Act
    C. results of applying agreed-upon procedures to an account within unaudited financial statements
    D. audit of historical financial statements

20. When an accountant compiles projected financial statements, the accountant's report should include a separate paragraph that
    A. describes the differences between a projection and a forecast
    B. identifies the accounting principles used by management
    C. expresses limited assurance that the actual results may be within the projection's range
    D. describes the limitations on the projection's usefulness

21. When an accountant examines a financial forecast that fails to disclose several significant assumptions used to prepare the forecast, the accountant should describe the assumptions in the accountant's report and issue a(n)
    A. "except for" qualified opinion
    B. "subject to" qualified opinion
    C. unqualified opinion with a separate explanatory paragraph
    D. adverse opinion

22. Soon after Boyd's audit report was issued, Boyd learned of certain related party transactions that occurred during the year under audit. These transactions were not disclosed in the notes to the financial statements. Boyd should
    A. plan to audit the transactions during the next engagement
    B. recall all copies of the audited financial statements
    C. determine whether the lack of disclosure would affect the auditor's report
    D. ask the client to disclose the transactions in subsequent interim statements

23. A former client requests a predecessor auditor to reissue an audit report on a prior period's financial statements. The financial statements are not restated and the report is not revised. What date(s) should the predecessor auditor use in the reissued report?
    A. The date of the prior-period report
    B. The date of the client's request
    C. The date of reissue
    D. The dual-dates

24. Management of Hill Company has decided not to account for a material transaction in accordance with the provisions of an FASB Standard. In setting forth its reasons in a note to the financial statements, management has clearly demonstrated that due to unusual circumstances, the financial statements presented in accordance with the FASB Standard would be misleading. The auditor's report should include a separate explanatory paragraph and contain a(n) _____ opinion.
    A. "except for" qualified
    B. "subject to" qualified
    C. adverse
    D. unqualified

25. If information accompanying the basic financial statements in an auditor-submitted document has been subjected to auditing procedures, the auditor may express an opinion that the accompanying information is fairly stated in
    A. conformity with generally accepting accounting principles
    B. all material respects in relation to the basic financial statements taken as a whole
    C. conformity with standards established by the AICPA
    D. accordance with generally accepted auditing standards

26. When using the work of a specialist, an auditor may refer to and identify the specialist in the auditor's report if the
    A. auditor wishes to indicate a division of responsibility
    B. specialist's work provides the auditor greater assurance of reliability
    C. auditor expresses an adverse opinion as a result of the specialist's findings
    D. specialist is not independent of the client

27. Negative confirmation of accounts receivable is less effective than positive confirmation of accounts receivable because
    A. a majority of recipients usually lack the willingness to respond objectively
    B. some recipients may report incorrect balances that require extensive follow-up
    C. the auditor cannot infer that all nonrespondents have verified their account information
    D. negative confirmations do not produce evidential matter that is statistically quantifiable

28. An auditor's program to examine long-term debt should include steps that require
    A. examining bond trust indentures
    B. inspecting the accounts payable subsidiary ledger
    C. investigating credits to the bond interest income account
    D. verifying the existence of the bondholders

29. Which of the following audit procedures would MOST likely assist an auditor in identifying conditions and events that may indicate there could be substantial doubt about an entity's ability to continue as a going concern?
    A. Review compliance with the terms of debt agreements
    B. Confirmation of accounts receivable from principal customers
    C. Reconciliation of interest expense with debt outstanding
    D. Confirmation of bank balances

30. Which of the following documentation is required for an audit in accordance with generally accepted auditing standards?
    A. An internal control questionnaire
    B. A client engagement letter
    C. A planning memorandum or checklist
    D. A client representation letter

31. When an accounting application is processed by computer, an auditor cannot verify the reliable operation of programmed control procedures by
    A. manually comparing detail transaction files used by an edit program to the program's generated error listing to determine that errors were properly identified by the edit program
    B. constructing a processing system for accounting applications and processing actual data from throughout the period through both the client's program and the auditor's program
    C. manually reperforming, as of a point in time, the processing of input data and comparing the simulated results to the actual results
    D. periodically submitting auditor-prepared test data to the same computer process and evaluating the results

32. To obtain evidence that user identification and password controls are functioning as designed, an auditor would MOST likely
    A. attempt to sign-on to the system using invalid user identifications and passwords
    B. write a computer program that simulates the logic of the client's access control software
    C. extract a random sample of processed transactions and ensure that the transactions were appropriately authorized
    D. examine statements signed by employees stating that they have not divulged their user identifications and passwords to any other person

33. While performing a substantive test of details during an audit, the auditor determined that the sample results supported the conclusion that the recorded account balance was materially misstated. It was, in fact, not materially misstated. This situation illustrates the risk of
    A. incorrect rejection
    B. incorrect acceptance
    C. overreliance
    D. underreliance

34. Which of the following would be designed to estimate a numerical measurement of a population, such as a dollar value?
    A. Sampling for variables
    B. Sampling for attributes
    C. Discovery sampling
    D. Numerical sampling

35. Before performing a review of a nonpublic entity's financial statement, an accountant should
    A. complete a series of inquiries concerning the entity's procedures for recording, classifying, and summarizing transactions
    B. apply analytical procedures to provide limited assurance that no material modifications should be made to the financial statements
    C. obtain a sufficient level of knowledge of the accounting principles and practices of the industry in which the entity operates
    D. inquire whether management has omitted substantially all of the disclosures required by generally accepted accounting principles

36. An auditor uses the knowledge provided by the understanding of the internal control structure and the assessed level of control risk primarily to
    A. determine whether procedures and records concerning the safeguarding of assets are reliable
    B. ascertain whether the opportunities to allow any person to both perpetrate and conceal irregularities are minimized
    C. modify the initial assessments of inherent risk and preliminary judgments about materiality levels
    D. determine the nature, timing, and extent of substantive tests for financial statement assertions

37. An auditor's flowchart of a client's accounting system is a diagrammatic representation that depicts the author's
    A. program for tests of controls
    B. understanding of the system
    C. understanding of the types of irregularities that are probable, given the present system
    D. documentation of the study and evaluation of the system

38. Computer systems are typically supported by a variety of utility software packages that are important to an auditor because they
    A. may enable unauthorized changes to data files if not properly controlled
    B. are very versatile programs that can be used on hardware of many manufacturers
    C. may be significant components of a client's application programs
    D. are written specifically to enable auditors to extract and sort data

39. When obtaining an understanding of an entity's control environment, an auditor should concentrate on the substance of management's policies and procedures rather than their form because
    A. the auditor may believe that the policies and procedures are inappropriate for that particular entity
    B. the board of directors may not be aware of management's attitude toward the control environment
    C. management may establish appropriate policies and procedures but not act on them
    D. the policies and procedures may be so weak that no reliance is contemplated by the auditor

40. After obtaining an understanding of an entity's internal control structure and assessing control risk, an auditor may next
    A. perform tests of controls to verify management's assertions that are embodied in the financial statements
    B. consider whether evidential matter is available to support a further reduction in the assessed level of control risk
    C. apply analytical procedures as substantive tests to validate the assessed level of control risk
    D. evaluate whether the internal control structure policies and procedures detected material misstatements in the financial statements

41. An auditor is LEAST likely to test the internal controls that provide for 41.____
    A. approval of the purchase and sale of marketable securities
    B. classification of revenue and expense transactions by product line
    C. segregation of the functions of recording disbursements and reconciling the bank account
    D. comparison of receiving reports and vendors' invoices with purchase orders

42. The possibility of erasing a large amount of information stored on magnetic tape MOST likely would be reduced by the use of 42.____
    A. file protection rings   B. check digits
    C. completeness tests   D. conversion verification

43. Which of the following MOST likely represents a weakness in the internal control structure of an EDP system? 43.____
    A. The systems analyst reviews output and controls the distribution of output from the EDP department.
    B. The accounts payable clerk prepares data for computer processing and enters the data into the computer.
    C. The systems programmer designs the operating and control functions of programs and participates in testing operating systems.
    D. The control clerk establishes control over data received by the EDP department and reconciles control totals after processing.

44. Evidential matter concerning proper segregation of duties ordinarily is BEST obtained by 44.____
    A. inspection of third-party documents containing the initials of who applied control procedures
    B. direct personal observation of the employee who applies control procedures
    C. preparation of a flowchart of duties performed and available personnel
    D. making inquiries of co-workers about the employee who applies control procedures

45. An internal control narrative indicates that an approved voucher is required to support every check request for payment of merchandise. Which of the following procedures provides the GREATEST assurance that this control is operating effectively? 45.____
    Select and examine
    A. vouchers and ascertain that the related cancelled checks are dated no later than the vouchers
    B. vouchers and ascertain that the related cancelled checks are dated no earlier than the vouchers
    C. cancelled checks and ascertain that the related vouchers are dated no earlier than the checks
    D. cancelled checks and ascertain that the related vouchers are dated no later than the checks

46. For effective internal control purposes, the vouchers payable department generally should
    A. stamp, perforate, or otherwise cancel supporting documentation after payment is mailed
    B. ascertain that each requisition is approved as to price, quantity, and quality by an authorized employee
    C. obliterate the quantity ordered on the receiving department copy of the purchase order
    D. establish the agreement of the vendor's invoice with the receiving report and purchase order

47. An auditor's tests of controls over the issuance of raw materials to production would MOST likely include
    A. reconciling raw materials and work in process perpetual inventory records to general ledger balances
    B. inquiring of the custodian about the procedures followed when defective materials are received from vendors
    C. observing that raw materials are stored in secure areas and that storeroom security is supervised by a responsible individual
    D. examining material requisitions and reperforming client controls designed to process and record issuances

48. A weakness in internal control over recording retirements of equipment may cause an auditor to
    A. trace additions to the "other assets" account to search for equipment that is still on hand but no longer being used
    B. select certain items of equipment from the accounting records and locate them in the plant
    C. inspect certain items of equipment in the plant and trace those items to the accounting records
    D. review the subsidiary ledger to ascertain whether depreciation was taken on each item of equipment during the year

49. The third general standard states that due care is to be exercised in the performance of an audit. This standard is generally interpreted to require
    A. objective review of the adequacy of the technical training and proficiency of firm personnel
    B. critical review of work done at every level of supervision
    C. thorough review of the existing internal control structure
    D. periodic review of a CPA firm's quality control procedures

50. An accountant's report expressing an opinion on an entity's internal controls should
    A. briefly explain the broad objectives and inherent limitations of internal control
    B. state that the study and evaluation of the internal controls was conducted in accordance with generally accepted auditing standards
    C. clearly disclaim responsibility for the establishment and maintenance of the internal controls
    D. include an opinion concerning management's assertions about whether the cost of correcting any material weaknesses would exceed the benefits of reducing the risk of errors and irregularities

50.____

51. An accountant has been engaged to report on an entity's internal controls without performing an audit of the financial statements. What restrictions, if any, should the accountant place on the use of this report?
    A. This report should be restricted for use by management.
    B. This report should be restricted for use by the audit committee.
    C. This report should be restricted for use by a specified regulatory agency.
    D. The accountant does not need to place any restrictions on the use of this report.

51.____

52. Which of the following combinations results in a decrease in sample size in a sample for attributes?

	Risk of overreliance	Tolerable rate	Expected poplation deviation rate
A.	Increase	Decrease	Increase
B.	Decrease	Increase	Decrease
C.	Increase	Increase	Decrease
D.	Increase	Increase	Increase

52.____

53. What is an auditor's evaluation of a statistical sample for attributes when a test of 100 documents results in 4 deviations if tolerable rate is 5%, the expected population deviation rate is 3%, and the allowance for sampling risk is 2%?
    A. Accept the sample results as support for planned reliance on the control because the tolerable rate less the allowance for sampling risk equals the expected population deviation rate.
    B. Modify planned reliance on the control because the sample deviation rate plus the allowance for sampling risk exceeds the tolerable rate.
    C. Modify planned reliance on the control because the tolerable rate plus the allowance for sampling risk exceeds the expected population deviation rate.
    D. Accept the sample results as support for planned reliance on the control because the sample deviation rate plus the allowance for sampling risk exceeds the tolerable rate.

53.____

54. A principal advantage of statistical methods of attribute sampling over non-statistical methods is that they provide a scientific basis for planning the
   A. risk of overreliance
   B. tolerable rate
   C. expected population deviation rate
   D. sample size

54.____

55. Which of the following symbolic representations indicates that new payroll transactions and the old payroll file have been used to prepare payroll checks, prepare a printed payroll journal, and generate a new payroll file?

55.____

A.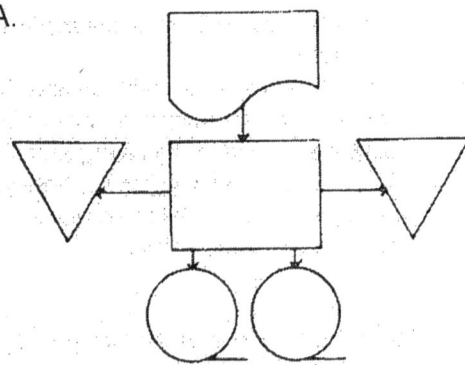

B.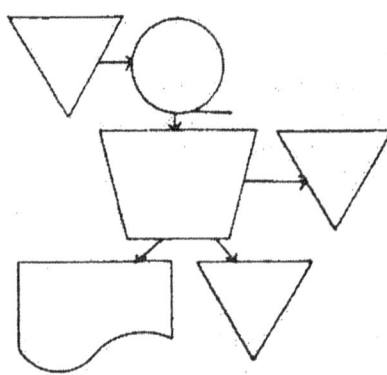

C.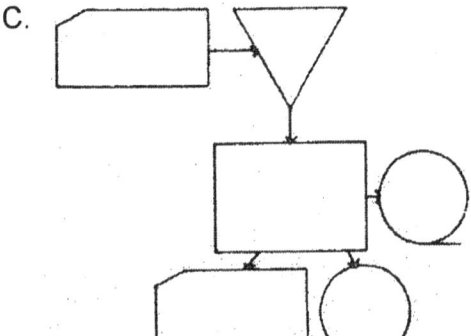

D.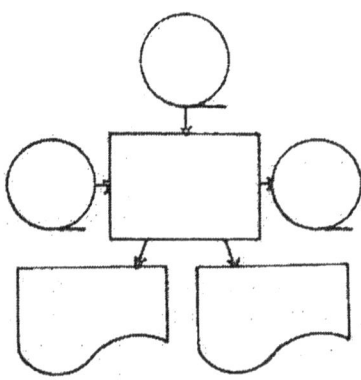

56. The profession's ethical standards would MOST likely be considered to have been violated when a CPA
   A. continued an audit engagement after the commencement of litigation against the CPA alleging excessive fees filed in a stockholders' derivative action
   B. represented to a potential client that the CPA's fees were substantially lower than he fees charged by other CPA's for comparable services
   C. issued a report on a financial forecast that omitted a caution regarding achievability
   D. accepted an MAS consultation engagement concerning data processing services for which the CPA lacked independence

56.____

57. If requested to perform a review engagement for a nonpublic entity in which an accountant has an immaterial direct financial interest, the accountant is
    A. independent because the financial interest is immaterial and, therefore, may issue a review report
    B. not independent and, therefore, may not be associated with the financial statements
    C. not independent and, therefore, may not issue a review report
    D. not independent and, therefore, may issue a review report, but may not issue an auditor's opinion

57.____

58. Reportable conditions are matters that come to an auditor's attention, which should be communicated to an entity's audit committee because they represent
    A. material irregularities or illegal acts perpetrated by high-level management
    B. significant deficiencies in the design or operation of the internal control structure
    C. flagrant violations of the entity's documented conflict-of-interest policies
    D. intentional attempts by client personnel to limit the scope of the auditor's field work

58.____

59. Which of the following factors is MOST important concerning an auditor's responsibility to detect errors and irregularities?
    A. The susceptibility of the accounting records to intentional manipulations, alterations, and the misapplication of accounting principles
    B. The probability that unreasonable accounting estimates result from unintentional bias or intentional attempts to misstate the financial statements
    C. The possibility that management fraud, defalcations, and the misappropriation of assets may indicate the existence of illegal acts
    D. The risk that mistakes, falsifications, and omissions may cause the financial statements to contain material misstatements

59.____

60. If specific information comes to an auditor's attention that implies the existence of possible illegal acts that could have a material, but indirect effect on the financial statements, the auditor should next
    A. apply audit procedures specifically directed to ascertaining whether an illegal act has occurred
    B. seek the advice of an informed expert qualified to practice law as to possible contingent liabilities
    C. report the matter to an appropriate level of management at least one level above those involved
    D. discuss the evidence with the client's audit committee, or others with equivalent authority and responsibility

60.____

KEY (CORRECT ANSWERS)

1. D	11. C	21. D	31. C	41. B	51. D
2. D	12. C	22. C	32. A	42. A	52. C
3. A	13. B	23. A	33. A	43. A	53. B
4. B	14. B	24. D	34. A	44. B	54. D
5. B	15. D	25. B	35. C	45. D	55. D
6. A	16. B	26. C	36. D	46. D	56. C
7. C	17. C	27. C	37. B	47. D	57. C
8. A	18. C	28. A	38. A	48. B	58. B
9. D	19. C	29. A	39. C	49. B	59. D
10. A	20. D	30. D	40. B	50. A	60. A

EXAMINATION SECTION

DIRECTIONS: Each question or incomplete statement is followed by several suggested answers or completions. Select the one that BEST answers the question or completes the statement. *PRINT THE LETTER OF THE CORRECT ANSWER IN THE SPACE AT THE RIGHT.*

1. Each of the following might, by itself, form a valid basis for an auditor to decide to omit a test EXCEPT for the
    A. difficulty and expense involved in testing a particular item
    B. degree of reliance on the relevant internal controls
    C. relative risk involved
    D. relationship between the cost of obtaining evidence and its usefulness

   1.____

2. Which of the following bodies promulgates standards for audits of federal financial assistance recipients?
    A. Governmental Accounting Standards Board
    B. Financial Accounting Standards Board
    C. General Accounting Office
    D. Governmental Auditing Standards Board

   2.____

3. According to the profession's ethical standards, an auditor would be considered independent in which of the following instances?
    A. The auditor's checking account, which is fully insured by a federal agency, is held at a client financial institution.
    B. The auditor is also an attorney who advises the client as its general counsel.
    C. An employee of the auditor donates service as treasurer of a charitable organization that is a client.
    D. The client owes the auditor fees for two consecutive annual audits.

   3.____

4. A CPA firm's quality control procedures pertaining to the acceptance of a prospective audit client would MOST likely include
    A. inquiry of management as to whether disagreements between the predecessor auditor and the prospective client were resolved satisfactorily
    B. consideration of whether sufficient competent evidential matter may be obtained to afford a reasonable basis for an opinion
    C. inquiry of third parties, such as the prospective client's bankers and attorneys, about information regarding the prospective client and its management
    D. consideration of whether the internal control structure is sufficiently effective to permit a reduction in the extent of required substantive tests

   4.____

5. Which of the following audit risk components may be assessed in nonquantitative terms?

	Inherent risk	Control risk	Detection risk
A.	Yes	Yes	No
B.	Yes	No	Yes
C.	No	Yes	Yes
D.	Yes	Yes	Yes

6. The development of constructive suggestions to a client for improvements in its internal control structure is
    A. addressed by the auditor only during a special engagement
    B. as important as establishing a basis for reliance on the internal control structure
    C. a requirement of the auditor's consideration of the internal control structure
    D. a desirable by-product of an audit engagement

7. Which of the following statements BEST describes how a detailed audit program of a CPA who is engaged to audit the financial statements of a large publicly held company compares with the audit client's comprehensive internal audit program?
    The comprehensive internal audit program is
    A. substantially identical to the audit program used by the CPA because both cover substantially identical areas
    B. less detailed and covers fewer areas than would normally be covered by the CPA
    C. more detailed and covers areas that would normally not be covered by the CPA
    D. more detailed although it covers fewer areas than would normally be covered by the CPA

8. As a result of tests of controls, an auditor overrelied on internal control and decreased substantive testing. This overreliance occurred because the true deviation rate in the population was
    A. less than the risk of overreliance on the auditor's sample
    B. less than the deviation rate in the auditor's sample
    C. more than the risk of overreliance on the auditor's sample
    D. more than the deviation rate in the auditor's sample

9. A procedure that would MOST likely be used by an auditor in performing tests of control procedures that involve segregation of functions and that leave no transaction trail is
    A. inspection
    B. observation
    C. reperformance
    D. reconciliation

10. Which of the following is NOT a reason an auditor should obtain an understanding of the elements of an entity's internal control structure in planning an audit?
    A. Identify the types of potential misstatements that can occur.
    B. Design substantive tests.
    C. Consider the operating effectiveness of the internal control structure.
    D. Consider factors that affect the risk of material misstatements.

    10.____

11. Which of the following is NOT an element of an entity's internal control structure?
    A. Control risk
    B. Control procedures
    C. The accounting system
    D. The control environment

    11.____

12. Errors in data processed in a batch computer system may NOT be detected immediately because
    A. transaction trails in a batch system are available only for a limited period of time
    B. there are time delays in processing transactions in a batch system
    C. errors in some transactions cause rejection of other transactions in the batch
    D. random errors are more likely in a batch system than in an on-line system

    12.____

13. When EDP programs or files can be accessed from terminals, users should be required to enter a(n)
    A. parity check
    B. personal identification code
    C. self-diagnosis test
    D. echo check

    13.____

14. When goods are received, the receiving clerk should match the goods with the
    A. purchase order and the requisition form
    B. vendor's invoice and the receiving report
    C. vendor's shipping document and the purchase order
    D. receiving report and the vendor's shipping document

    14.____

15. The mailing of disbursement checks and remittance advices should be controlled by the employee who
    A. signed the checks list
    B. approved the vouchers for payment
    C. matched the receiving reports, purchase orders, and vendors' invoices
    D. verified the mathematical accuracy of the vouchers and remittance advices

    15.____

16. An auditor who is testing EDP controls in a payroll system would MOST likely use test data that contain conditions such as
    A. deductions not authorized by employees
    B. overtime not approved by supervisors
    C. time tickets with invalid job numbers
    D. payroll checks with unauthorized signatures

    16.____

17. The purpose of segregating the duties of hiring personnel and distributing payroll checks is to separate the
    A. administrative controls from the internal accounting controls
    B. human resources function from the controllership function
    C. operational responsibility from the record keeping responsibility
    D. authorization of transactions from the custody of related assets

17.____

18. Independent internal verification of inventory occurs when employees who
    A. issue raw materials obtain material requisitions for each issue and prepare daily totals of materials issued
    B. compare records of goods on hand with physical quantities do not maintain the records or have custody of the inventory
    C. obtain receipts for the transfer of completed work to finished goods prepare a completed production report
    D. are independent of issuing production orders update records from completed job cost sheets and production cost reports on a timely basis

18.____

19. When there are numerous property and equipment transactions during the year, an auditor planning to assess control risk at the minimum level usually plans to obtain an understanding of the internal control structure and to perform
    A. tests of controls and extensive tests of property and equipment balances at the end of the year
    B. extensive tests of current year property and equipment transactions
    C. tests of controls and limited tests of current year property and equipment transactions
    D. analytical procedures for property and equipment balances at the end of the year

19.____

20. Which of the following statements is CORRECT concerning an auditor's communication of internal control structure related matters (reportable conditions) noted in an audit?
    A. The auditor may issue a written report to the audit committee representing that no reportable conditions were noted during the audit.
    B. Reportable conditions should be recommunicated each year even if the audit committee has acknowledged its understanding of such deficiencies
    C. Reportable conditions may not be communicated in a document that contains suggestions regarding activities that concern other topics such as business strategies or administrative efficiencies.
    D. The auditor may choose to communicate significant internal control structure related matters either during the course of the audit or after the audit is concluded.

20.____

21. An accountant's report expressing an opinion on an entity's internal controls should contain a
    A. statement that the entity's internal controls are consistent with that of the prior year after giving effect to subsequent changes
    B. brief explanation of the broad objectives and inherent limitations of internal control
    C. description of the principal controls that protect assets against loss from unauthorized use or disposition
    D. statement that the engagement was conducted in accordance with generally accepted auditing standards

22. An independent accountant, without auditing an entity's financial statements, may accept an engagement to express an opinion on the entity's internal controls in effect

	As of a specified date	During a specified period of time
A.	Yes	Yes
B.	Yes	No
C.	No	Yes
D.	No	No

23. An auditor who uses statistical sampling for attributes in testing internal controls should reduce the planned reliance on a prescribed control when the
    A. sample rate of deviation is less than the expected rate of deviation used in planning the sample
    B. tolerable rate less the allowance for sampling risk exceeds the sample rate of deviation
    C. sample rate of deviation plus the allowance for sampling risk exceeds the tolerable rate
    D. sample rate of deviation plus the allowance for sampling risk equals the tolerable rate

24. Which of the following factors is generally NOT considered in determining the sample size for a test of controls?
    A. Population size
    B. Tolerable rate
    C. Risk of overreliance
    D. Expected population deviation rate

25. An advantage of using statistical over nonstatistical sampling methods in tests of controls is that the statistical methods
    A. afford greater assurance than a nonstatistical sample of equal size
    B. provide an objective basis for quantitatively evaluating sample risks
    C. can more easily convert the sample into a dual-purpose test for substantive testing
    D. eliminate the need to use judgment in determining appropriate sample sizes

26. The concept of materiality would be LEAST important to an auditor when considering the
    A. effects of a direct financial interest in the client upon the CPA's independence
    B. decision whether to use positive or negative confirmations of accounts receivable
    C. adequacy of disclosure of a client's illegal act
    D. discovery of weaknesses in a client's internal control structure

27. The primary objective of analytical procedures used in the final review stage of an audit is to
    A. obtain evidence from details tested to corroborate particular assertions
    B. identify areas that represent specific risks relevant to the audit
    C. assist the auditor in assessing the validity of the conclusions reached
    D. satisfy doubts when questions arise about a client's ability to continue in existence

28. To help plan the nature, timing, and extent of substantive auditing procedures, preliminary analytical procedures should focus on
    A. enhancing the auditor's understanding of the client's business and events that have occurred since the last audit date
    B. developing plausible relationships that corroborate anticipated results with a measurable amount of precision
    C. applying ratio analysis to externally generated data such as published industry statistics or price indices
    D. comparing recorded financial information to the results of other tests of transactions and balances

29. Cooper, CPA, is auditing the financial statements of a small rural municipality. the receivable balances represent residents' delinquent real estate taxes. The internal control structure at the municipality is weak. To determine the existence of the accounts receivable balances at the balance sheet date, Cooper would MOST likely
    A. send positive confirmation requests
    B. send negative confirmation requests
    C. examine evidence of subsequent cash receipts
    D. inspect the internal records such as copies of the tax invoices that were mailed to the residents

30. An auditor would MOST likely verify the interest earned on bond investments by
    A. vouching the receipt and deposit of interest checks
    B. confirming the bond interest rate with the issuer of the bonds
    C. recomputing the interest earned on the basis of face amount, interest rate, and period held
    D. testing the internal controls over cash receipts

31. Which of the following MOST likely would be detected by an auditor's review of a client's sales cut-off?
    A. Unrecorded sales for the year
    B. Lapping of year-end accounts receivable
    C. Excessive sales discounts
    D. Unauthorized goods returned for credit

32. Auditors should request that an audit client send a letter of inquiry to those attorneys who have been consulted concerning litigation, claims, or assessments. The PRIMARY reason for this request is to provide
    A. information concerning the progress of cases to date
    B. corroborative evidential matter
    C. an estimate of the dollar amount of the probable loss
    D. an expert opinion as to whether a loss is possible, probable, or remote

33. Tracing selected items from the payroll register to employee time cards that have been approved by supervisory personnel provides evidence that
    A. internal controls relating to payroll disbursements were operating effectively
    B. payroll checks were signed by an appropriate officer independent of the payroll preparation process
    C. only bona fide employees worked and their pay was properly computed
    D. employees worked the number of hours for which their pay was computed

34. A written client representation letter MOST likely would be an auditor's best source of corroborative information of a client's plans to
    A. terminate an employee pension plan
    B. make a public offering of its common stock
    C. settle an outstanding lawsuit for an amount less than the accrued loss contingency
    D. discontinue a line of business

35. In an audit of contingent liabilities, which of the following procedures would be LEAST effective?
    A. Reviewing a bank confirmation letter
    B. Examining customer confirmation replies
    C. Examining invoices for professional services
    D. reading the minutes of the board of directors

Questions 36-37.

DIRECTIONS: Questions 36 and 37 are to be answered on the basis of the following information.

Miles Company
Bank Transfer Schedule
December 31, 2015

Check Number	Bank Accounts		Amount	Date Disbursed Per		Date Deposited Per	
	From	To		Books	Bank	Books	Bank
2020	1st Natl.	Suburban	$32,000	12/31	1/5♦	12/31	1/3♦
2021	1st Natl.	Capital	21,000	12/31	1/4♦	12/31	1/3♦
3217	2nd State	Suburban	6,700	1/3	1/5	1/3	1/6
0659	Midtown	Suburban	5,500	12/30	1/5♦	12/30	1/3♦

36. The tick mark (♦) MOST likely indicates that the amount was traced to the 36.____
   A. December cash disbursements journal
   B. outstanding check list of the applicable bank reconciliation
   C. January cash disbursements journal
   D. year-end bank confirmations

37. The tick mark (♦) MOST likely indicates that the amount was traced to the 37.____
   A. deposits in transit of the applicable bank reconciliation
   B. December cash receipts journal
   C. January cash receipts journal
   D. year-end bank confirmations

38. Which of the following is NOT a major reason why an accounting audit trail should be maintained for a computer system? 38.____
   A. Monitoring purposes
   B. Analytical procedures
   C. Query answering
   D. Deterrent to irregularities

39. Which of the following computer-assisted auditing techniques allows fictitious and real transactions to be processed together without client operating personnel being aware of the testing process? 39.____
   A. Parallel simulation
   B. Generalized audit software programming
   C. Integrated test facility
   D. Test data approach

40. In a probability-proportional-to-size sample with a sampling interval of $10,000, an auditor discovered that a selected account receivable with a recorded amount of $5,000 had an audit amount of $2,000. The projected error of this sample was 40.____
   A. $3,000   B. $4,000   C. $6,000   D. $8,000

41. An auditor is performing substantive tests of pricing and extensions of perpetual inventory balances consisting of a large number of items. Past experience indicates numerous pricing and extension errors. Which of the following statistical sampling approaches is MOST appropriate?
    A. Unstratified mean-per-unit
    B. Probability-proportional-to-size
    C. Stop or go
    D. Ratio estimation

    41.____

42. An auditor searching for related party transactions should obtain an understanding of each subsidiary's relationship to the total entity because
    A. this may permit the audit of intercompany account balances to be performed as of concurrent dates
    B. intercompany transactions may have been consummated on terms equivalent to arm's-length transactions
    C. this may reveal whether particular transactions would have taken place if the parties had not been related
    D. the business structure may be deliberately designed to obscure related party transactions

    42.____

43. A typical objective of an operational audit is to determine whether an entity's
    A. internal control structure is adequately operating as designed
    B. operational information is in accordance with generally accepted governmental auditing standards
    C. financial statements present fairly the results of operations
    D. specific operating units are functioning efficiently and effectively

    43.____

44. An auditor concludes that the omission of a substantive procedure considered necessary at the time of the examination may impair the auditor's present ability to support the previously expressed opinion. The auditor need not apply the omitted procedure if the
    A. risk of adverse publicity or litigation is low
    B. results of other procedures that were applied tend to compensate for the procedure omitted
    C. auditor's opinion was qualified because of a departure from generally accepted accounting principles
    D. results of the subsequent period's tests of controls make the omitted procedure less important

    44.____

45. One of the conditions required for an accountant to submit a written personal financial plan containing unaudited financial statements to a client without complying with the requirements of SSARS 1 (Compilation and Review of Financial Statements) is that the
    A. client agrees that the financial statements will not be used to obtain credit
    B. accountant compiled or reviewed the client's financial statements for the immediate prior year
    C. engagement letter acknowledges that the financial statements will contain departures from generally accepted accounting principles
    D. accountant expresses limited assurance that the financial statements are free of any material misstatements

    45.____

46. A limitation on the scope of an auditor's examination sufficient to preclude an unqualified opinion will always result when management
    A. engages the auditor after the year-end physical inventory count is completed
    B. fails to correct a material internal control weakness that had been identified during the prior year's audit
    C. refuses to furnish a management representation letter to the auditor
    D. prevents the auditor from reviewing the working papers of the predecessor auditor

47. An accountant has been asked to compile the financial statements of a nonpublic company on a prescribed form that omits substantially all the disclosures required by generally accepted accounting principles. If the prescribed form is a standard preprinted form adopted by the company's industry trade association, and is to be transmitted only to such associations, the accountant
    A. need not advise the industry trade association of the omission of all disclosures
    B. should disclose the details of the omissions in separate paragraphs of the compilation report
    C. is precluded from issuing a compilation report when all disclosures are omitted
    D. should express limited assurance that the financial statements are free of material misstatements

48. On September 30, 2015, Miller was asked to reissue an auditor's report, dated March 31, 2015, on a client's financial statements for the year ended December 31, 2014. Miller will submit the reissued report to the client in a document that contains information in addition to the client's basic financial statements. However, Miller discovered that the client suffered substantial losses on receivables resulting from conditions that occurred since March 31, 2015. Miller should
    A. request the client to disclose the event in a separate, appropriately labeled note to the financial statements and reissue the original report with its original date
    B. request the client to restate the financial statements and reissue the original report with a dual date
    C. reissue the original report with its original date without regard to whether the event is disclosed in a separate note to the financial statements
    D. not reissue the original report but issue a "subject to" qualified opinion that discloses the event in a separate explanatory paragraph

49. An auditor who qualifies an opinion because of an insufficiency of evidential matter should describe the limitation in an explanatory paragraph. The auditor should also refer to the limitation in the

	Scope paragraph	Opinion paragraph	Notes to the financial statements
A.	Yes	No	Yes
B.	No	Yes	No
C.	Yes	Yes	No
D.	Yes	Yes	Yes

50. An auditor who conducts an examination in accordance with generally accepted auditing standards and concludes that the financial statements are fairly presented in accordance with a comprehensive basis of accounting other than generally accepted accounting principles, such as the cash basis of accounting, should issue a
    A. special report
    B. disclaimer of opinion
    C. review report
    D. qualified opinion

51. An auditor concludes that there is a material inconsistency in the other information in an annual report to shareholders containing audited financial statements. If the auditor concludes that the financial statements do not require revision, but the client refuses to revise or eliminate the material inconsistency, the auditor may
    A. issue an "except for" qualified opinion after discussing the matter with the client's board of directors
    B. consider the matter closed since the other information is not in the audited financial statements
    C. disclaim an opinion on the financial statements after explaining the material inconsistency in a separate explanatory paragraph
    D. revise the auditor's report to include a separate explanatory paragraph describing the material inconsistency

52. An auditor may NOT issue a qualified opinion when
    A. a scope limitation prevents the auditor from completing an important audit procedure
    B. the auditor's report refers to the work of a specialist
    C. an accounting principle at variance with generally accepted accounting principles is used
    D. the auditor lacks independence with respect to the audited entity

53. Comfort letters ordinarily are addressed to
    A. The Securities and Exchange Commission
    B. underwriters of securities
    C. creditor financial institutions
    D. the client's audit committee

54. Unaudited financial statements for the prior year presented in comparative form with audited financial statements for the current year should be clearly marked to indicate their status and
   I. the report on the prior period should be reissued to accompany the current period report
   II. the report on the current period should include as a separate paragraph a description of the responsibility assumed for the prior period's financial statements

   The CORRECT answer is:
   A. I only
   B. II only
   C. both I and II
   D. either I or II

   54.____

55. When a publicly-held company refuses to include in its audited financial statements any of the segment information that the auditor believes is required, the auditor should issue a(n)
   A. unqualified opinion with a separate explanatory paragraph emphasizing the matter
   B. "except for" qualified opinion because of inadequate disclosure
   C. adverse opinion because of the lack of conformity with generally accepted accounting principles
   D. disclaimer of opinion because of the significant scope limitation

   55.____

56. Green Company uses the first-in, first-out method of costing for its international subsidiary's inventory and the last-in, first-out method of costing for its domestic inventory. The different costing methods would cause Green's auditor to issue a report with an
   A. explanatory paragraph as to consistency
   B. "except for" qualified opinion
   C. opinion modified as to consistency
   D. unqualified opinion

   56.____

57. An accountant's standard report on a compilation of a projection should NOT include a
   A. separate paragraph that describes the limitations on the presentation's usefulness
   B. statement that a compilation of a projection is limited in scope
   C. disclaimer of responsibility to update the report for events occurring after the report's date
   D. statement that the accountant expresses only limited assurance that the results may be achieved

   57.____

58. An accountant may accept an engagement to apply agreed-upon procedures to prospective financial statements provided that
    A. distribution of the report is to be restricted to the specified users involved
    B. the prospective financial statements are also examined
    C. responsibility for the adequacy of the procedures performed is taken by the accountant
    D. negative assurance is expressed on the prospective financial statements taken as a whole

58.____

59. When a client will not permit inquiry of outside legal counsel, the audit report will ordinarily contain a(n)
    A. disclaimer of opinion
    B. "except for" qualified opinion
    C. "subject to" qualified opinion
    D. unqualified opinion with a separate explanatory paragraph

59.____

60. An auditor may issue the standard audit report when the
    A. auditor refers to the findings of a specialist
    B. financial statements are derived and condensed from complete audited financial statements that are filed with a regulatory agency
    C. financial statements are prepared on the cash receipts and disbursements basis of accounting
    D. principal auditor assumes responsibility for the work of another auditor

60.____

KEY (CORRECT ANSWERS)

1.	A	11.	A	21.	B	31.	A	41.	D	51.	D
2.	C	12.	B	22.	A	32.	B	42.	D	52.	D
3.	A	13.	B	23.	C	33.	D	43.	D	53.	B
4.	C	14.	C	24.	A	34.	D	44.	B	54.	D
5.	D	15.	A	25.	B	35.	B	45.	A	55.	B
6.	D	16.	C	26.	A	36.	B	46.	C	56.	D
7.	C	17.	D	27.	C	37.	A	47.	A	57.	D
8.	D	18.	B	28.	A	38.	B	48.	A	58.	A
9.	B	19.	C	29.	A	39.	C	49.	C	59.	A
10.	C	20.	D	30.	C	40.	C	50.	A	60.	D

EXAMINATION SECTION

DIRECTIONS: Each question or incomplete statement is followed by several suggested answers or completions. Select the one that BEST answers the question or completes the statement. *PRINT THE LETTER OF THE CORRECT ANSWER IN THE SPACE AT THE RIGHT.*

1. An accountant who is NOT independent of a client is precluded from issuing a
   A. compilation report on historical financial statements
   B. compilation report on prospective financial statements
   C. special report on compliance with contractual agreements
   D. report on management advisory services

   1.____

2. Which of the following elements underlies the application of generally accepted auditing standards, particularly the standards of field work and reporting?
   A. Internal accounting control
   B. Corroborating evidence
   C. Quality control
   D. Materiality and relative risk

   2.____

3. Which of the following acts by a CPA who is not in public practice would MOST likely be considered a violation of the ethical standards of the profession?
   A. Using the CPA designation without disclosing employment status in connection with financial statements issued for external uses by the CPA's employer
   B. Distributing business cards indicating the CPA designation and the CPA's title and employer
   C. Corresponding on the CPA's employer's letterhead, which contains the CPA designation and the CPA's employment status
   D. Compiling the CPA's employer's financial statements and making reference to the CPA's lack of independence

   3.____

4. The ethical standards of the profession would MOST likely be considered to be violated if a CPA
   A. owns a building and leases a portion of the space to an audit client
   B. has an insured account with a brokerage firm that is an audit client and the account is used for occasional cash transactions
   C. is asked by an audit client to act as a "finder" in the acquisition of another company on a per diem basis
   D. searches for and initially screens candidates for the vacant controllership of an audit client

   4.____

5. Which of the following statements BEST explains why the CPA profession has found it essential to promulgate ethical standards and to establish means for ensuring their observance?
   A. Vigorous enforcement of an established code of ethics is the best way to prevent unscrupulous acts
   B. Ethical standards that emphasize excellence in performance over material rewards establish a reputation for competence and character
   C. A distinguishing mark of a profession is its acceptance of responsibility to the public
   D. A requirement for a profession is to establish ethical standards that stress primarily a responsibility to clients and colleagues

6. Which of the following procedures would an auditor MOST likely include in the initial planning of an examination of financial statements?
   A. Discussing the examination with firm personnel responsible for non-audit services to the client
   B. Inquiring of the client's attorney as to any claims probable of assertion
   C. Obtaining a written representation letter from management of the client
   D. Determining whether necessary internal accounting control procedures are being applied as prescribed

7. The audit work performed by each assistant should be reviewed to determine whether it was adequately performed and to evaluate whether the
   A. audit procedures performed are approved in the professional standards
   B. examination has been performed by persons having adequate technical training and proficiency as auditors
   C. auditor's system of quality control has been maintained at a high level
   D. results are consistent with the conclusions to be presented in the auditor's report

8. Which of the following procedures would an auditor ordinarily perform during the review of subsequent events?
   A. An analysis of related party transactions for the discovery of possible irregularities
   B. A review of the cut-off bank statements for the period after the year-end
   C. An inquiry of the client's legal counsel concerning litigation
   D. An investigation of material weaknesses in internal accounting control previously communicated to the client

9. Which of the following circumstances would MOST likely cause an auditor to suspect that material irregularities exist in a client's financial statements?
   A. Property and equipment are usually sold at a loss before being fully depreciated.
   B. Significantly fewer responses to confirmation requests are received than expected.
   C. Monthly bank reconciliations usually include several in-transit items.
   D. Clerical errors are listed on an EDP-generated exception report.

10. An auditor's tests of the pricing of a client's inventory indicates the existence of many errors. However, because of inadequate records the auditor is uncertain about whether these errors materially affect the financial statements taken as a whole. The auditor may reasonably issue a(n)

	"Subject to" qualified opinion	Adverse opinion
A.	Yes	Yes
B.	Yes	No
C.	No	Yes
D.	No	No

10.____

11. A CPA firm should establish procedures for conducting and supervising work at all organizational levels to provide reasonable assurance that the work performed meets the firm's standards of quality. To achieve this goal, the firm MOST likely would establish procedures for
   A. evaluating prospective and continuing client relationships
   B. reviewing engagement working papers and reports
   C. requiring personnel to adhere to the applicable independence rules
   D. maintaining personnel files containing documentation related to the evaluation of personnel

11.____

12. An auditor of a manufacturer would MOST likely question whether that client has committed illegal acts if the client has
   A. been forced to discontinue operations in a foreign country
   B. been an annual donor to a local political candidate
   C. failed to correct material weaknesses in internal accounting control that were reported after the prior year's audit
   D. disclosed several subsequent events involving foreign operations in the notes to the financial statements

12.____

13. The purpose of compliance tests is to provide reasonable assurance that
   A. internal accounting control procedures are being applied as prescribed
   B. the extent of substantive testing is kept to a minimum
   C. errors and irregularities are prevented or detected in a timely manner
   D. the auditor has an understanding of the control environment

13.____

14. The Securities and Exchange Commission has authority to
   A. prescribe specific auditing procedures to detect fraud concerning inventories and accounts receivable of companies engaged in interstate commerce
   B. deny lack of privity as a defense in third-party actions for gross negligence against the auditors of public companies
   C. determine accounting principles for the purpose of financial reporting by companies offering securities to the public
   D. require a change of auditors of governmental entities after a given period of years as a means of ensuring auditor independence

14.____

15. Which of the following standard applies to management advisory services engagements?
    A. In all matters relating to the assignment, an independence in mental attitude is to be maintained.
    B. There is to be a proper study and evaluation of the existing internal accounting control as a basis for reliance thereon.
    C. The work is to be adequately planned and assistants are to be properly supervised.
    D. Informative disclosures are to be regarded as reasonably adequate unless otherwise stated in the report.

16. An auditor's report includes the following statement: "The financial statements do not present fairly the financial position, results of operations, or cash flows in conformity with generally accepted accounting principles." This auditor's report was MOST likely issued in connection with financial statements that are
    A. inconsistent
    B. based on prospective financial information
    C. misleading
    D. affected by a material uncertainty

17. An auditor includes a middle paragraph in an otherwise unqualified report to emphasize that the financial statements are not comparable to those of prior years due to a court-ordered divestiture that is already fully explained in the notes to the financial statements. The inclusion of this paragraph
    A. should be followed by an "except for" consistency modification in the opinion paragraph
    B. requires a revision of the opinion paragraph to include the phrase "with the foregoing explanation"
    C. is not appropriate and may confuse the readers or lead them to believe the report was qualified
    D. is appropriate and would not negate the unqualified opinion

18. Green, CPA, is requested to render an opinion on the application of accounting principles by an entity that is audited by another CPA. Green may
    A. not accept such an engagement because to do so would be considered unethical
    B. not accept such an engagement because Green would lack the necessary information on which to base an opinion without conducting an audit
    C. accept the engagement but should form an independent opinion without consulting with the continuing CPA
    D. accept the engagement but should consult with the continuing CPA to ascertain all the available facts relevant to forming a professional judgment

19. An auditor may reasonably issue an "except for" qualified opinion for

	Inadequate disclosure	Scope limitation
A.	Yes	Yes
B.	Yes	No
C.	No	Yes
D.	No	No

19.____

20. An auditor may reasonably issue a "subject to" qualified opinion for

	Lack of consistency	Departure from generally accepted accounting principles
A.	Yes	Yes
B.	Yes	No
C.	No	Yes
D.	No	No

20.____

21. An auditor did not examine an entity's financial statements for the preceding year. Inadequate financial records precluded an opinion as to asset and liability balances at the beginning of the current year and the consistent application of generally accepted accounting principles. The auditor should explain the inadequacies in the financial records in
    A. a middle paragraph, the lack of consistency in the opinion paragraph, and express a disclaimer of opinion on the financial statements
    B. a middle paragraph, the lack of consistency also in the middle paragraph, and express an opinion only on the balance sheet
    C. the opinion paragraph, the lack of consistency also in the opinion paragraph, and express a disclaimer of opinion on the financial statements
    D. the opinion paragraph, the lack of consistency also in the opinion paragraph, and express an opinion only on the balance sheet

21.____

22. Each page of a nonpublic entity's financial statements reviewed by an accountant should include the following reference.
    A. See Accountant's Review Report
    B. Reviewed. No Accountant's Assurance Expressed
    C. See Accompanying Accountant's Footnotes
    D. Reviewed. No Material Modifications Required

22.____

23. An auditor's document includes the following statement: "Our audit is subject to the risk that errors, irregularities, or illegal acts, including fraud or defalcations, if they exist, will not be detected. However, we will inform you of any such matters that come to our attention."
The above passage is MOST likely from
    A. the explanatory paragraph of a "subject to" qualified auditor's report
    B. an engagement letter
    C. the explanatory paragraph of a compliance report on a governmental entity subject to GAO standards
    D. a comfort letter

23.____

24. An accountant may accept an engagement to apply agreed-upon procedures that are not sufficient to express an opinion on one or more specified accounts or items of a financial statement provided that
    A. the accountant's report does not enumerate the procedures performed
    B. the financial statements are prepared in accordance with a comprehensive basis of accounting other than generally accepted accounting principles
    C. distribution of the accountant's report is restricted
    D. the accountant is also the entity's continuing auditor

25. Reports are considered special reports when issued in connection with
    A. compliance with aspects of regulatory requirements related to audited financial statements
    B. pro forma financial presentations designed to demonstrate the effect of hypothetical transactions
    C. feasibility studies presented to illustrate an entity's results of operations
    D. interim financial information reviewed to determine whether material modifications should be made to conform with generally accepted accounting principles

26. When an accountant issues to an underwriter a comfort letter containing comments on data that have not been audited, the underwriter MOST likely will receive
    A. positive assurance on supplementary disclosures
    B. negative assurance on capsule information
    C. a disclaimer on prospective financial statements
    D. a limited opinion on "pro forma" financial statements

27. Prospective financial information presented in the format of historical financial statements that omit either gross profit or net income is deemed to be a
    A. partial presentation
    B. projected balance sheet
    C. financial forecast
    D. financial projection

28. After an audit report containing an unqualified opinion on a non-public client's financial statements was issued, the client decided to sell the shares of a subsidiary that accounts for 30% of its revenue and 25% of its net income. The auditor should
    A. determine whether the information is reliable and, if determined to be reliable, request that revised financial statements be issued
    B. notify the entity that the auditor's report may no longer be associated with the financial statements
    C. describe the effects of this subsequently discovered information in a communication with persons known to be relying on the financial statements
    D. take no action because the auditor has no obligation to make any further inquiries

29. The principal auditor is satisfied with the independence and professional reputation of the other auditor who has audited the financial statements of a subsidiary. To indicate the division of responsibility, the principal auditor should modify
    A. only the opinion paragraph of the report
    B. only the opinion paragraph of the report and include an explanatory middle paragraph
    C. only the scope paragraph of the report
    D. both the scope and opinion paragraphs of the report

29.____

30. An accountant should not submit unaudited financial statements to the management of a nonpublic company unless, at a minimum, the accountant
    A. assists in adjusting the books of account and prepares a trial balance
    B. types or reproduces the financial statements on plain paper
    C. complies with the standards applicable to compilation engagements
    D. applies analytical procedures to the financial statements

30.____

31. In evaluating internal accounting control, the auditor is basically concerned that the system provides reasonable assurance that
    A. operational efficiency has been achieved in accordance with management plans
    B. errors and irregularities have been prevented or detected
    C. controls have not been circumvented by collusion
    D. management cannot override the system

31.____

32. Proper segregation of functional responsibilities in an effective system of internal accounting control calls for separation of the functions of
    A. authorization, execution, and payment
    B. authorization, recording, and custody
    C. custody, execution, and reporting
    D. authorization, payment, and recording

32.____

33. A basic objective of a CPA firm is to provide professional services that conform with professional standards. Reasonable assurance of achieving this basic objective is provided through
    A. compliance with generally accepting reporting standards
    B. a system of quality control
    C. a system of peer review
    D. continuing professional education

33.____

34. When performing the review of an internal accounting control system's design, an auditor may obtain answers to an internal accounting control questionnaire. The next step ordinarily should be to
    A. make a preliminary evaluation of whether specific control procedures are suitably designed for reliance, assuming satisfactory compliance
    B. perform compliance tests to provide reasonable assurance that the control procedures are being applied as prescribed
    C. gather enough evidence to determine if the internal accounting control system is effective in preventing or detecting errors and irregularities
    D. design substantive tests that do not contemplate reliance on the control procedures that appear to be ineffective

34.____

35. An auditor's study and evaluation of the internal accounting control system made in connection with an annual audit is usually not sufficient to express an opinion on an entity's system because
    A. the evaluation of weaknesses is subjective enough that an auditor should not express an opinion on the internal accounting controls alone
    B. the audit cost-benefit relationship permits an auditor to express only reasonable assurance that the system operates as designed
    C. management may change the internal accounting controls to correct weaknesses
    D. only those controls on which an auditor intends to rely are reviewed, tested, and evaluated

35.____

36. Which of the following characteristics distinguishes computer processing from manual processing?
    A. Computer processing virtually eliminates the occurrence of computational error normally associated with manual processing.
    B. Errors or irregularities in computer processing will be detected soon after their occurrence.
    C. The potential for systematic error is ordinarily greater in manual processing than in computerized processing.
    D. Most computer systems are designed so that transaction trails useful for audit purposes do not exist.

36.____

37. After an auditor prepared a flowchart of the internal accounting controls relating to sales and evaluated the design of the system, the auditor would perform compliance tests on all internal accounting control procedures
    A. that would aid in preventing irregularities
    B. documented in the flowchart
    C. considered to be weaknesses that might allow errors to enter the accounting system
    D. considered to be strengths that the auditor plans to rely on

37.____

38. Which of the following would MOST likely be a weakness in the internal accounting control system of a client that utilizes microcomputers rather than a larger computer system?
    A. Employee collusion possibilities are increased because microcomputers from one vendor can process the programs of a system from a different vendor.
    B. The microcomputer operators may be able to remove hardware and software components and modify them at home.
    C. Programming errors result in all similar transactions being processed incorrectly when those transactions are processed under the same conditions.
    D. Certain transactions may be automatically initiated by the microcomputers and management's authorization of these transactions may be implicit in its acceptance of the system design.

39. During the review of a small business client's internal accounting control system, the auditor discovered that the accounts receivable clerk approves credit memos and has access to cash. Which of the following controls would be MOST effective in offsetting this weakness?
    A. The owner reviews errors in billings to customers and postings to the subsidiary ledger.
    B. The controller receives the monthly bank statement directly and reconciles the checking accounts.
    C. The owner reviews credit memos after they are recorded.
    D. The controller reconciles the total of the detail accounts receivable accounts to the amount shown in the ledger.

40. At which point in an ordinary sales transaction of a wholesaling business would a lack of specific authorization LEAST concern the auditor conducting an audit?
    A. Determining discounts
    B. Selling goods for cash
    C. Granting credit
    D. Shipping goods

41. Cash receipts from sales on account have been misappropriated. Which of the following acts would conceal this defalcation and be LEAST likely to be detected by an auditor?
    A. Understating the sales journal
    B. Overstating the accounts receivable control account
    C. Overstating the accounts receivable subsidiary ledger
    D. Understating the cash receipts journal

42. For effective internal accounting control, the accounts payable department should compare the information on each vendor's invoice with the
    A. receiving report and the purchase order
    B. receiving report and the voucher
    C. vendor's packing slip and the purchase order
    D. vendor's packing slip and the voucher

43. Which of the following is the MOST effective control procedure to detect vouchers that were prepared for the payment of goods that were not received?
    A. Count goods upon receipt in storeroom
    B. Match purchase order, receiving report, and vendor's invoice for each voucher in accounts payable department
    C. Compare goods received with goods requisitioned in receiving department
    D. Verify vouchers for accuracy and approval in internal audit department

44. Which of the following control procedures would MOST likely be used to maintain accurate perpetual inventory records?
    A. Independent storeroom count of goods received
    B. Periodic independent reconciliation of control and subsidiary records
    C. Periodic independent comparison of records with goods on hand
    D. Independent matching of purchase orders, receiving reports, and vendors' invoices

45. If a control total were to be computed on each of the following data items, which would BEST be identified as a hash total for a payroll EDP application?
    A. Hours worked
    B. Total debits and total credits
    C. Net pay
    D. Department numbers

46. Which of the following procedures is MOST likely to prevent the improper disposition of equipment?
    A. A separation of duties between those authorized to dispose of equipment and those authorized to approve removal work orders
    B. The use of serial numbers to identify equipment that could be sold
    C. Periodic comparison of removal work orders to authorizing documentation
    D. A periodic analysis of the scrap sales and the repairs and maintenance accounts

47. Which of the following statements is CORRECT concerning the auditor's required communication of a material weakness in internal accounting control?
    A. A weakness that management refuses to correct should be included in a separate paragraph of the auditor's report.
    B. A weakness previously communicated during the prior year's audit that has not been corrected should be communicated again in writing.
    C. Suggested corrective action for management's consideration concerning a weakness need not be communicated to the client.
    D. The auditor should test for compliance any weakness discovered before communicating it to the client.

48. A CPA has performed an examination of the general purpose financial statements of Big City. The examination scope included the additional requirements of the Single Audit Act. When reporting on Big City's internal accounting and administrative controls used in administering a federal financial assistance program, the CPA should
    A. communicate those weaknesses that are material in relation to the general purpose financial statements
    B. express an opinion on the systems used to administer major federal financial assistance programs and express negative assurance on the systems used to administer nonmajor federal financial assistance programs
    C. communicate those weaknesses that are material in relation to the federal financial assistance program
    D. express negative assurance on the systems used to administer major federal financial assistance programs and express no opinion on the systems used to administer nonmajor federal financial assistance programs

48.____

49. Which of the following conclusions could an auditor MOST likely make on completing the preliminary phase of the review of internal accounting control?
    A. Specific control procedures are suitably designed for the auditor to rely on to restrict the extent of substantive tests, assuming satisfactory compliance.
    B. The audit effort required to study and evaluate the design of the system exceeds the reduction in audit effort that could be achieved by reliance on the system.
    C. The accounting control procedures are suitably designed to provide reasonable assurance that errors and irregularities will be prevented or detected, provided functions are properly segregated.
    D. Compliance tests indicate that access to computer operations is so unrestricted that the internal accounting control system cannot be relied on to restrict the extent of substantive tests.

49.____

50. During a compilation of a nonpublic entity's financial statements, an accountant would be LEAST likely to
    A. omit substantially all of the disclosures required by generally accepted accounting principles
    B. issue a compilation report on one or more, but not all of the basic financial statements
    C. perform analytical procedures designed to identify relationships that appear to be unusual
    D. read the compiled financial statements and consider whether they appear to include adequate disclosure

50.____

51. A basic premise underlying analytical review procedures is that
    A. these procedures cannot replace tests of balances and transactions
    B. statistical tests of financial information may lead to the discovery of material errors in the financial statements
    C. the study of financial ratios is an acceptable alternative to the investigation of unusual fluctuations
    D. relationships among data may reasonably be expected to exist and continue in the absence of known conditions to the contrary

52. An auditor who uses the work of a specialist may refer to and identify the specialist in the auditor's report if the
    A. specialist is also considered to be a related party
    B. auditor indicates a division of responsibility related to the work of the specialist
    C. specialist's work provides the auditor greater assurance of reliability
    D. auditor expresses an "except for" qualified opinion or an adverse opinion related to the work of the specialist

53. An auditor should obtain evidential matter relevant to all of the following factors concerning third-party litigation against a client EXCEPT the
    A. period in which the underlying cause for legal action occurred
    B. probability of an unfavorable outcome
    C. jurisdiction in which the matter will be resolved
    D. existence of a situation indicating an uncertainty as to the possible loss

54. An auditor analyzes repairs and maintenance accounts primarily to obtain evidence in support of the audit assertion that all
    A. noncapitalizable expenditures for repairs and maintenance have been properly charged to expense
    B. expenditures for property and equipment have not been charged to expense
    C. noncapitalizable expenditures for repairs and maintenance have been recorded in the proper period
    D. expenditures for property and equipment have been recorded in the proper period

55. For which of the following account balances are substantive tests of details LEAST likely to be performed unless analytical review procedures indicate the need to extend detail testing?
    A. Payroll expense
    B. Marketable securities
    C. Research and development costs
    D. Legal expense

56. Which of the following statements concerning working papers is INCORRECT? 56.____
    A. An auditor may support an opinion by other means in addition to working papers.
    B. The form of working papers should be designed to meet the circumstances of a particular engagement.
    C. An auditor's working papers may not serve as a reference source for the client.
    D. Working papers should show that the internal accounting control system has been studied and evaluated to the degree necessary.

57. The two requirements crucial to achieving audit efficiency and effectiveness 57.____
    with a microcomputer are selecting
    A. the appropriate audit tasks for microcomputer applications and the appropriate software to perform the selected audit tasks
    B. the appropriate software to perform the selected audit tasks and client data that can be accessed by the auditor's microcomputer
    C. client data that can be accessed by the auditor's microcomputer and audit procedures that are generally applicable to several clients in a specific industry
    D. audit procedures that are generally applicable to several clients in a specific industry and the appropriate audit tasks for microcomputer applications

58. Compiled financial statements should be accompanied by a report stating all 58.____
    of the following EXCEPT
    A. the accountant does not express an opinion or any other form of assurance on the financial statements
    B. a compilation is substantially less in scope than an examination in accordance with generally accepted auditing standards
    C. the accountant compiled the financial statements in accordance with standards established by the AICPA
    D. a compilation is limited to presenting in the form of financial statements information that is the representation of management

59.

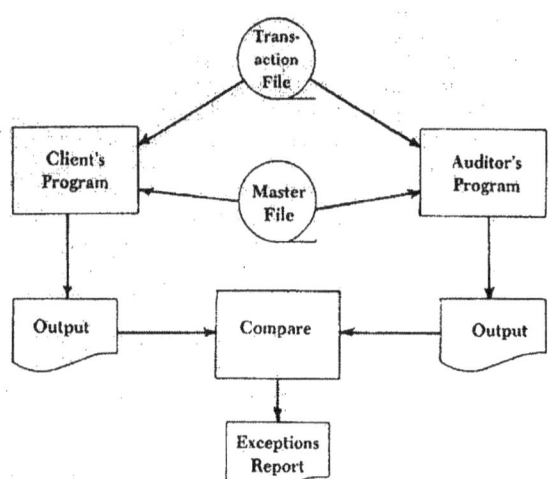

The above flowchart depicts
A. program code checking
B. parallel simulation
C. integrated test facility
D. controlled reprocessing

60.

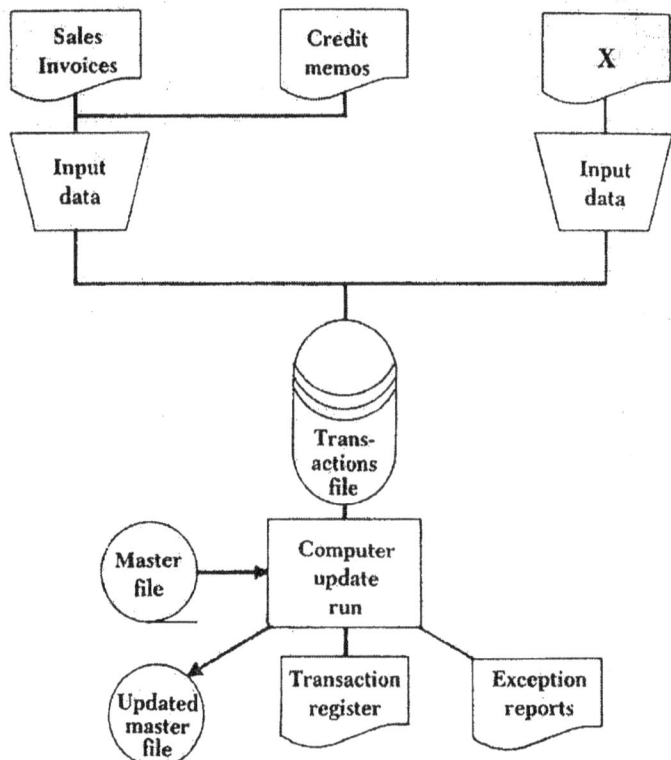

In a credit sales and cash receipts system flowchart, symbol X could represent
A. auditor's test data
B. remittance advices
C. error reports
D. credit authorization forms

KEY (CORRECT ANSWERS)

1. C	11. B	21. B	31. B	41. A	51. D
2. D	12. A	22. A	32. B	42. A	52. D
3. A	13. A	23. B	33. B	43. B	53. C
4. A	14. C	24. C	34. A	44. C	54. B
5. C	15. C	25. A	35. D	45. D	55. A
6. A	16. C	26. B	36. A	46. A	56. C
7. D	17. D	27. A	37. D	47. C	57. A
8. C	18. D	28. D	38. B	48. C	58. B
9. B	19. A	29. D	39. C	49. B	59. B
10. D	20. D	30. C	40. B	50. C	60. B

EXAMINATION SECTION
TEST 1

DIRECTIONS: Each question or incomplete statement is followed by several suggested answers or completions. Select the one that BEST answers the question or completes the statement. *PRINT THE LETTER OF THE CORRECT ANSWER IN THE SPACE AT THE RIGHT.*

1. After studying and evaluating a client's system of internal accounting control, an auditor has concluded that the system is well designed and is functioning as intended. Under these circumstances, the auditor would MOST likely
    A. perform compliance tests to the extent outlined in the audit program
    B. determine the control procedures that should prevent or detect errors and irregularities
    C. not increase the extent of predetermined substantive tests
    D. determine whether transactions are recorded to permit preparation of financial statements in conformity with generally accepted accounting principles

2. When considering the objectivity of internal auditors, an independent auditor should
    A. evaluate the quality control program in effect for the internal auditors
    B. examine documentary evidence of the work performed by the internal auditors
    C. test a sample of the transactions and balances that the internal auditors examined
    D. determine the organizational level to which the internal auditors report

3. Which of the following statements is NOT true of the test data approach when testing a computerized accounting system?
    A. The test data need consist of only those valid and invalid conditions which interest the auditor.
    B. Only one transaction of each type need be tested.
    C. The test data must consist of all possible valid and invalid conditions.
    D. Test data are processed by the client's computer programs under the auditor's control.

4. After the preliminary phase of the review of a client's EDP controls, an auditor may decide not to perform compliance tests related to the control procedures within the EDP portion of the client's internal accounting control system. Which of the following would NOT be a valid reason for choosing to omit compliance tests?
    A. The controls duplicate operative controls existing elsewhere in the system.
    B. There appear to be major weaknesses that would preclude reliance on the stated procedure.
    C. The time and dollar costs of testing exceed the time and dollar savings in substantive testing if the compliance tests show the controls to be operative.
    D. The controls appear adequate.

5. The objectives of internal accounting control for a production cycle are to provide assurance that transactions are properly executed and recorded, and that
   A. custody of work in process and of finished goods is properly maintained
   B. production orders are prenumbered and signed by a supervisor
   C. raw materials purchases are authorized by the purchasing department
   D. independent internal verification of activity reports is established

6. An auditor performs a test to determine whether all merchandise for which the client was billed was received. The population for this test consists of all
   A. merchandise received
   B. vendors' invoices
   C. canceled checks
   D. receiving reports

7. Internal accounting control is ineffective when computer department personnel
   A. participate in computer software acquisition decisions
   B. design documentation for computerized systems
   C. originate changes in master files
   D. provide physical security for program files

8. An auditor may compensate for a weakness in the internal accounting control system by increasing the
   A. level of detection risk
   B. extent of compliance testing
   C. preliminary judgment about audit risk
   D. extent of analytical review procedures

9. Internal accounting control is strengthened when the quantity of merchandise ordered is omitted from the copy of the purchase order sent to the
   A. department that initiated the requisition
   B. receiving department
   C. purchasing agent
   D. accounts payable department

10. Property acquisitions that are misclassified as maintenance expense would MOST likely be detected by an internal accounting control system that provides for
    A. investigation of variances within a formal budgeting system
    B. review and approval of the monthly depreciation entry by the plant supervisor
    C. segregation of duties of employees in the accounts payable department
    D. examination by the internal auditor of vendor invoices and canceled checks for property acquisitions

11. Sound internal accounting control procedures dictate that defective merchandise returned by customers should presented to the _____ clerk.
    A. inventory control
    B. sales
    C. purchasing
    D. receiving

12. Which of the following procedures MOST likely would be included as part of an auditor's tests of compliance?
    A. Inspection
    B. Reconciliation
    C. Confirmation
    D. Analytical review

13. An effective system of internal accounting control over the payroll function would include
    A. verification of agreement of job time tickets with employee clock card hours by a payroll department employee
    B. reconciliation of totals on job time tickets with job reports by employees responsible for those specific jobs
    C. custody of rate authorization records by the supervisor of the payroll department
    D. preparation of payroll transaction journal entries by an employee who reports to the supervisor of the personnel department

14. What is an auditor's responsibility to communicate a material weakness in internal accounting control discovered in interim work for the current year's audit that the auditor had discovered and communicated to the client in the prior year's audit?
    A. The auditor should request a meeting with management at least one level above the department in which the weakness exists to discuss the reasons the weakness has not been corrected.
    B. The auditor should communicate this weakness to the client immediately because the discovery of such a weakness in internal accounting control is the purpose of the auditor's interim work.
    C. The auditor has no responsibility to again communicate with the client but should extend the audit procedures to investigate whether this weakness has any effect on the current year's financial statements.
    D. The auditor should communicate this weakness to the client either at the interim date or after completing the examination.

15. A CPA's report expressing an opinion on an entity's internal accounting control system identified several material weaknesses and will be published in the entity's annual report to shareholders. Management intends to include a statement asserting that the cost of correcting the weaknesses would exceed the benefits of reducing the risk of errors and irregularities. The CPA should
    A. insist that management's statement not appear in the same document as the CPA's report
    B. investigate whether the cost of correcting the weaknesses would, in fact, exceed the benefits
    C. insist that management correct the weaknesses if cost is the only consideration
    D. not express any opinion as to management's statement

16. A CPA's study and evaluation of the system of internal accounting control in an audit will generally
    A. be the same as that made in connection with an engagement to express an opinion on the system of internal accounting control
    B. result in the CPA expressing an opinion on the system of internal accounting control
    C. be more limited than that made in connection with an engagement to express an opinion on the system of internal accounting control
    D. be more extensive than that made in connection with an engagement to express an opinion on the system of internal accounting control

17. Using microcomputers in auditing may affect the methods used to review the work of staff assistants because
    A. supervisory personnel may not have an understanding of the capabilities and limitations of microcomputers
    B. working paper documentation may not contain readily observable details of calculations
    C. the audit field work standards for supervision may differ
    D. documenting the supervisory review may require assistance of management services personnel

18. Which of the following statistical sampling plans does not use a fixed sample size for compliance testing purposes?
    A. Dollar-unit sampling
    B. Sequential sampling
    C. PPS sampling
    D. Variables sampling

19. Which of the following factors does an auditor generally need to consider in planning a particular audit sample for a compliance test?
    A. Number of items in the population
    B. Total dollar amount of the items to be sampled
    C. Acceptable level of risk of overreliance
    D. Tolerable error

20. Which of the following procedures in the cash disbursements cycle should NOT be performed by the accounts payable department?
    A. Comparing the vendor's invoice with the receiving report
    B. Canceling supporting documentation after payment
    C. Verifying the mathematical accuracy of the vendor's invoice
    D. Signing the voucher for payment by an authorized person

21. Which of the following statements is generally correct about the competence of evidential matter?
    A. The auditor's direct personal knowledge, obtained through observation and inspection, is more persuasive than information obtained indirectly from independent outside sources.
    B. To be competent, evidential matter must be either valid or relevant, but need not be both.
    C. Accounting data alone may be considered sufficient competent evidential matter to issue an unqualified opinion on financial statements.
    D. Competence of evidential matter refers to the amount of corroborative evidence to be obtained.

22. To establish the existence and ownership of a long-term investment in the common stock of a publicly-traded company, an auditor ordinarily performs a security count or
    A. relies on the client's internal accounting controls if the auditor has reasonable assurance that the control procedures are being applied as prescribed
    B. confirms the number of shares owned that are held by an independent custodian
    C. determines the market price per share at the balance sheet date from published quotations
    D. confirms the number of shares owned with the issuing company

23. If a client maintains perpetual inventory records in quantities and in dollars, and its internal accounting control over inventory is weak, an auditor would probably
    A. apply gross profit tests to ascertain the reasonableness of the physical counts
    B. increase the extent of compliance tests of the inventory cycle
    C. request the client to schedule the physical inventory count at the end of the year
    D. insist that the client perform physical counts of inventory items several times during the year

24. An auditor testing long-term investments would ordinarily use analytical review as the primary audit procedure to ascertain the reasonableness of the
    A. valuation of marketable equity securities
    B. classification of gains and losses on the disposal of securities
    C. completeness of recorded investment income
    D. existence and ownership of investments

25. An auditor reporting on comparative financial statements is not required to include an explanatory paragraph in the auditor's report if the opinion paragraph is modified because of a(n)
    A. change in accounting principle
    B. scope limitation
    C. disclaimer of opinion
    D. uncertainty affecting the financial statements

26. Which of the following cash transfers results in a misstatement of cash at December 31, 2015?

Bank Transfer Schedule

	Disbursement		Receipt	
Transfer	Recorded in Books	Paid by Bank	Recorded in Books	Received by Bank
A.	12/31/14	1/4/15	12/31/14	12/31/14
B.	1/4/15	1/5/15	12/31/14	1/4/15
C.	12/31/14	1/5/15	12/31/14	1/4/14
D.	1/4/15	1/11/15	1/4/15	1/4/15

27. An auditor should trace corporate stock issuances and treasury stock transactions to the
    A. numbered stock certificates
    B. articles of incorporation
    C. transfer agent's records
    D. minutes of the board of directors

28. Which of the following procedures would an auditor MOST likely rely on to verify management's assertion of completeness?
    A. Review standard bank confirmations for indications of kiting
    B. Compare a sample of shipping documents to related sales invoices
    C. Observe the client's distribution of payroll checks
    D. Confirm a sample of recorded receivables by direct communication with the debtors

29. Working papers ordinarily would NOT include
    A. initials of the in-charge auditor indicating review of the staff assistant's work
    B. cut-off bank statements received directly from the banks
    C. a memo describing the preliminary review of the internal accounting control system
    D. copies of client inventory count sheets

30. When providing limited assurance that the financial statements of a non-public entity require no material modifications to be in accordance with generally accepted accounting principles, the accountant should
    A. understand the system of internal accounting control that the entity uses
    B. test the accounting records that identify inconsistencies with the prior year's financial statements
    C. understand the accounting principles of the industry in which the entity operates
    D. develop audit programs to determine whether the entity's financial statements are fairly presented

31. Processing data through the use of simulated files provides an auditor with information about the reliability of controls. One of the techniques involved in this approach makes use of
    A. controlled reprocessing
    B. integrated test facility
    C. input validation
    D. program code checking

32. Which of the following statements is CORRECT concerning statistical sampling in compliance testing?
    A. The population size has little or no effect on determining sample size except for very small populations.
    B. The expected population deviation rate has little or no effect on determining sample size except for very small populations.
    C. As the population size doubles, the sample size also should double.
    D. For a given tolerable rate, a larger sample size should be selected as the expected population deviation rate decreases.

33. A number of factors influences the sample size for a substantive test of details of an account balance. All other factors being equal, which of the following would lead to a larger sample size?
    A. Greater reliance on internal accounting controls
    B. Greater reliance on analytical review procedures
    C. Smaller expected frequency of errors
    D. Smaller measure of tolerable error

34. Which of the following statements is CORRECT concerning the auditor's use of statistical sampling?
    A. An auditor needs to estimate the dollar amount of the standard deviation of the population to use classical variables sampling.
    B. An assumption of PPS sampling is that the underlying accounting population is normally distributed.
    C. A classical variables sample needs to be designed with special considerations to include negative balances in the sample.
    D. The selection of zero balances usually does not require special sample design considerations when using PPS sampling.

35. Which of the following statements is CORRECT concerning related party transactions?
    A. In the absence of evidence to the contrary, related party transactions should be assumed to be outside the ordinary course of business.
    B. An auditor should determine whether a particular transaction would have occurred if the parties had not been related.
    C. An auditor should substantiate that related party transactions were consummated on terms equivalent to those that prevail in arm's-length transactions.
    D. The audit procedures directed toward identifying related party transactions should include considering whether transactions are occurring, but are not being given proper accounting recognition.

36. Ajax Company's auditor concludes that the omission of an audit procedure considered necessary at the time of the prior examination impairs the auditor's present ability to support the previously expressed unqualified opinion. If the auditor believes there are stockholders currently relying on the opinion, the auditor should promptly
    A. notify the stockholders currently relying on the previously expressed unqualified opinion that they should not rely on it
    B. advise management to disclose this development in its next interim report to the stockholders
    C. advise management to revise the financial statements with full disclosure of the auditor's inability to support the unqualified opinion
    D. undertake to apply the omitted procedure or alternate procedures that would provide a satisfactory basis for the opinion

37. A governmental audit may extend beyond an examination leading to the expression of an opinion on the fairness of financial presentation to include

	Program Results	Compliance	Economy & Efficiency
A.	Yes	Yes	No
B.	Yes	Yes	Yes
C.	No	Yes	Yes
D.	Yes	No	Yes

38. Which of the following procedures would an auditor MOST likely perform to obtain evidence about an entity's subsequent events?
    A. Reconcile bank activity for the month after the balance sheet date with cash activity reflected in the accounting records.
    B. Examine on a test basis the purchase invoices and receiving reports for several days after the inventory date.
    C. Review the treasurer's monthly reports on temporary investments owned, purchased, and sold.
    D. Obtain a letter from the entity's attorney describing any pending litigation, unasserted claims, or loss contingencies.

39. The current file of the auditor's working papers generally should include
    A. a flowchart of the internal accounting controls
    B. organization charts
    C. a copy of the financial statements
    D. copies of bond and note indentures

40. Which of the following procedures is NOT usually performed by the accountant in a review engagement of a nonpublic entity?
    A. Communicating any material weaknesses discovered during the study and evaluation of internal accounting control.
    B. Reading the financial statements to consider whether they conform with generally accepted accounting principles.
    C. Writing an engagement letter to establish an understanding regarding the services to be performed.
    D. Issuing a report stating that the review was performed in accordance with standards established by the AICPA.

41. An auditor did not observe a client's taking of beginning physical inventory and was unable to become satisfied about the inventory by means of other auditing procedures. Assuming no other scope limitations or reporting problems, the auditor could issue an unqualified opinion on the current year's financial statements for
    A. the balanced sheet only
    B. the income statement only
    C. the income and retained earnings statements only
    D. all of the financial statements

42. Performing inquiry and analytical procedures is the primary basis for an accountant to issue a(n)
    A. compilation report on financial statements for a nonpublic entity in its first year of operations
    B. review report on comparative financial statements for a nonpublic entity in its second year of operations
    C. management advisory report prepared at the request of a client's audit committee
    D. internal accounting control report for a governmental agency in accordance with GAO standards

43. Which of the following representations does an auditor make explicitly and which implicitly when issuing an unqualified opinion?

	Conformity With GAAP	Adequacy of Disclosure
A.	Explicitly	Explicitly
B.	Implicitly	Implicitly
C.	Implicity	Explicitly
D.	Explicity	Implicitly

44. The fourth standard of reporting requires the auditor's report to contain either an expression of opinion regarding the financial statements taken as a whole or an assertion to the effect that an opinion cannot be expressed. The objective of the fourth standard is to prevent
    A. an auditor from expressing different opinions on each of the basic financial statements
    B. restrictions on the scope of the examination, whether imposed by the client or by the inability to obtain evidence
    C. misinterpretations regarding the degree of responsibility the auditor is assuming
    D. an auditor from reporting on one basic financial statement and not the others

44.____

45. An auditor's report expresses an unqualified opinion and includes a middle paragraph that emphasizes a matter included in the notes to the financial statements. The auditor's report would be deficient if the middle paragraph states that the entity
    A. has changed from the completed-contract method to the percentage of completion method of accounting for long-term construction contracts
    B. has had a significant subsequent event
    C. has accounting reclassifications that enhance the comparability between the current and prior year
    D. is a component of a larger business enterprise

45.____

46. "Provision has been made for any material loss that might be sustained as a result of purchase commitments for inventory quantities in excess of normal requirements or at prices in excess of the prevailing market prices." The foregoing passage is MOST likely from
    A. a management representation letter
    B. the explanatory paragraph of an "except for" qualified auditor's report
    C. a vendor representation letter
    D. the explanatory paragraph of a "subject to" qualified auditor's report

46.____

47. For a particular entity's financial statements to be presented fairly in conformity with generally accepted accounting principles, it is NOT required that the principles selected
    A. be appropriate in the circumstances for the particular entity
    B. reflect transactions in a manner that presents the financial statements within a range of acceptable limits
    C. present information in the financial statements that is classified and summarized in a reasonable manner
    D. be applied on a basis consistent with those followed in the prior year

47.____

11 (#1)

48. Which of the following circumstances requires modification of the accountant's report on a review of interim financial information of a publicly-held entity?

	An Uncertainty	Inadequate Disclosure
A.	Yes	Yes
B.	No	No
C.	Yes	No
D.	No	Yes

49. An auditor's report issued in connection with which of the following is generally NOT considered to be a special report?
    A. Compliance with aspects of contractual agreements unrelated to audited financial statements
    B. Specified elements, accounts, or items of a financial statement presented in a document
    C. Financial statements prepared in accordance with an entity's income tax basis
    D. Financial information presented in a prescribed schedule that requires a prescribed form of auditor's report

50. Information accompanying the basic financial statements in an auditor-submitted document should NOT include a(n)
    A. analysis of inventory by location
    B. statement that the allowance for doubtful accounts is adequate
    C. statement that the depreciable life of a new asset is 20 years
    D. analysis of revenue by product line

51. The exercise of due professional care requires that an auditor
    A. use error-free judgment
    B. study and review internal accounting control, including compliance tests
    C. critically review the work done at every level of supervision
    D. examine all corroborating evidence available

52. Under which of the following circumstances would the independence of a CPA be considered impaired if the CPA, who is also an attorney, serves as auditor and provides legal services to the same client?
    A. When the CPA, as legal agent, consummates a business acquisition for the client
    B. When the CPA's audit fees and legal fees are not billed separately
    C. When the CPA uses legal expertise to research a question of income tax law
    D. When the legal services consist of an analysis of the terms of a lease agreement

53. A violation of the profession's ethical standards would MOST likely have occurred when a CPA
    A. purchased a bookkeeping firm's practice of monthly write-ups for a percentage of fees received ove4r a three-year period
    B. made arrangements with a bank to collect notes issued by a client in payment of fees due
    C. named Smith formed a partnership with two other CPA's and use "Smith &Co." as the firm name
    D. issued an unqualified opinion on the 2015 financial statements when fees for the 2014 audit were unpaid

54. Before accepting an audit engagement, a successor auditor should make specific inquiries of the predecessor auditor regarding the predecessor's
    A. awareness of the consistency in the application of generally accepted accounting principles between periods
    B. evaluation of all matters of continuing accounting significance
    C. opinion of any subsequent events occurring since the predecessor's audit report was issued
    D. understanding as to the reasons for the change of auditors

55. When planning an examination, an auditor should
    A. consider whether the extent of substantive tests may be reduced based on the results of the internal control questionnaire
    B. make preliminary judgments about materiality levels for audit purposes
    C. conclude whether changes in compliance with prescribed control procedures justifies reliance on them
    D. prepare a preliminary draft of the management representation letter

56. A difference of opinion regarding the results of a sample cannot be resolved between the assistant who performed the auditing procedures and the in-charge auditor. The assistant should
    A. refuse to perform any further work on the engagement
    B. accept the judgment of the more experienced in-charge auditor
    C. document the disagreement and ask to be disassociated from the resolution of the matter
    D. notify the client that a serious audit problem exists

57. A CPA firm studies its personnel advancement experience to ascertain whether individuals meeting stated criteria are assigned increased degrees of responsibility. This is evidence of the firm's adherence to prescribed standards of
    A. supervision and review
    B. continuing professional education
    C. professional development
    D. quality control

58. An entity's financial statements were misstated over a period of years due to large amounts of revenue being recorded in journal entries that involved debits and credits to an illogical combination of accounts. The auditor could MOST likely have been alerted to his irregularity by
    A. scanning the general journal for unusual entries
    B. performing a revenue cut-off test at year-end
    C. tracing a sample of journal entries to the general ledger
    D. examining documentary evidence of sales returns and allowances recorded after year-end

59. The refusal of a client's attorney to provide a representation on the legality of a particular act committed by the client is generally
    A. sufficient reason to issue a "subject to" qualified opinion
    B. considered to be a scope limitation
    C. insufficient reason to modify the auditor's report due to the attorney's obligation of confidentiality
    D. proper grounds to withdraw from the engagement

60. If compiled financial statements presented in conformity with the cash receipts and disbursements basis of accounting do not disclose the basis of accounting used, the accountant should
    A. disclose the basis in the notes to the financial statements
    B. clearly label each page "Unaudited"
    C. disclose the basis of accounting in the accountant's report
    D. recompile the financial statements using generally accepted accounting principles

KEY (CORRECT ANSWERS)

1.	C	11.	D	21.	A	31.	B	41.	A	51.	C
2.	D	12.	A	22.	B	32.	A	42.	B	52.	A
3.	C	13.	A	23.	C	33.	D	43.	D	53.	D
4.	D	14.	D	24.	C	34.	A	44.	C	54.	D
5.	A	15.	D	25.	A	35.	D	45.	A	55.	B
6.	B	16.	C	26.	B	36.	D	46.	A	56.	C
7.	C	17.	B	27.	D	37.	B	47.	D	57.	D
8.	D	18.	B	28.	B	38.	D	48.	D	58.	A
9.	B	19.	C	29.	B	39.	C	49.	A	59.	B
10.	A	20.	B	30.	C	40.	A	50.	B	60.	C

INTERPRETING STATISTICAL DATA
GRAPHS, CHARTS AND TABLES
EXAMINATION SECTION
TEST 1

DIRECTIONS: Each questioner incomplete statement is followed by several suggested answers or completions. Select the one that BEST answers the question or completes the statement. *PRINT THE LETTER OF THE CORRECT ANSWER IN THE SPACE AT THE RIGHT.*

Questions 1-3.

DIRECTIONS: Questions 1 through 3 are to be answered SOLELY on the basis of the following table.

QUARTERLY SALES REPORTED BY MAJOR INDUSTRY GROUPS

DECEMBER 2021 – FEBRUARY 2023
Reported Sales, Taxable & Non-Taxable (in Millions)

Industry Groups	12/21-2/22	3/22-5/22	6/22-8/22	9/22-11/22	12/22-2/23
Retailers	2,802	2,711	2,475	2,793	2,974
Wholesalers	2,404	2,237	2,269	2,485	2,974
Manufacturers	3,016	2,888	3,001	3,518	3,293
Services	1,034	1,065	984	1,132	1,092

1. The trend in total reported sales may be described as
    A. downward
    B. downward and upward
    C. horizontal
    D. upward

2. The two industry groups that reveal a similar seasonal pattern for the period December 2021 through November 2022 are
    A. retailers and manufacturers
    B. retailers and wholesalers
    C. wholesalers and manufacturers
    D. wholesalers and service

3. Reported sales were at a MINIMUM between
    A. December 2021 and February 2022
    B. March 2022 and May 2022
    C. June 2022 and August 2022
    D. September 2022 and November 2022

89

TEST 2

DIRECTIONS: Each question or incomplete statement is followed by several suggested answers or completions. Select the one that BEST answers the question or completes the statement. *PRINT THE LETTER OF THE CORRECT ANSWER IN THE SPACE AT THE RIGHT*

Questions 1-4.

DIRECTIONS: Questions 1 through 4 are to be answered SOLELY on the basis of the following information.

The income elasticity of demand for selected items of consumer demand in the United States are:

Item	Elasticity
Airline Travel	5.66
Alcohol	.62
Dentist Fees	1.00
Electric Utilities	3.00
Gasoline	1.29
Intercity Bus	1.89
Local Bus	1.41
Restaurant Meals	.75

1. The demand for the item listed below that would be MOST adversely affected by a decrease in income is

   A. alcohol
   B. electric utilities
   C. gasoline
   D. restaurant meals

2. The item whose relative change in demand would be the same as the relative change in income would be

   A. dentist fees
   B. gasoline
   C. restaurant meals
   D. none of the above

3. If income increases by 12 percent, the demand for restaurant meals may be expected to increase by

   A. 9 percent
   B. 12 percent
   C. 16 percent
   D. none of the above

4. On the basis of the above information, the item whose demand would be MOST adversely affected by an increase in the sales tax from 7 percent to 8 percent to be passed on to the consumer in the form of higher prices

   A. would be airline travel
   B. would be alcohol
   C. would be gasoline
   D. cannot be determined

TEST 3

DIRECTIONS: Each question or incomplete statement is followed by several suggested answers or completions. Select the one that BEST answers the question or completes the statement. *PRINT THE LETTER OF THE CORRECT ANSWER IN THE SPACE AT THE RIGHT.*

Questions 1-3.

DIRECTIONS: Questions 1 through 3 are to be answered SOLELY on the basis of the following graphs depicting various relationships in a single retail store.

GRAPH 1
RELATIONSHIP BETWEEN NUMBER OF CUSTOMERS STORE AND TIME OF DAY

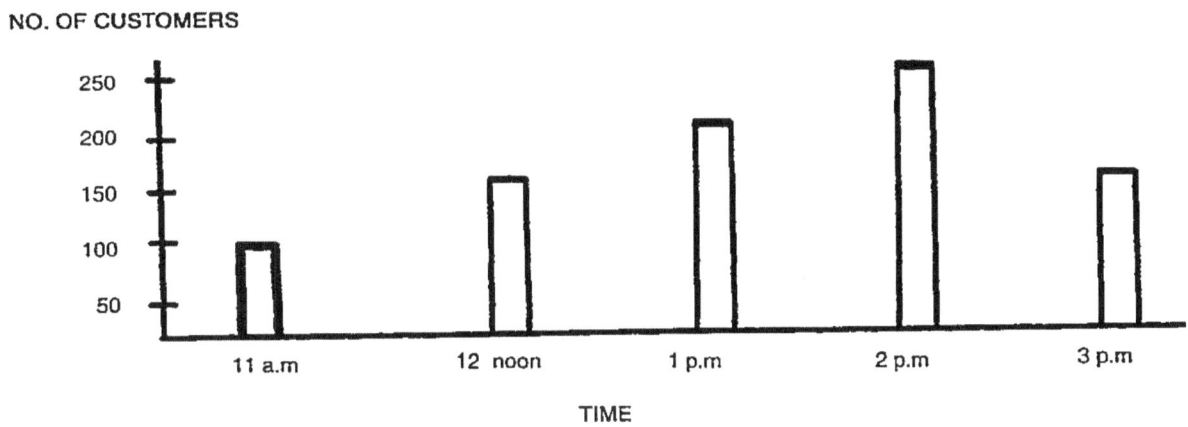

GRAPH II
RELATIONSHIP BETWEEN NUMBER OF CHECK-OUT LANES AVAILABLE IN STORE AND WAIT TIME FOR CHECK-OUT

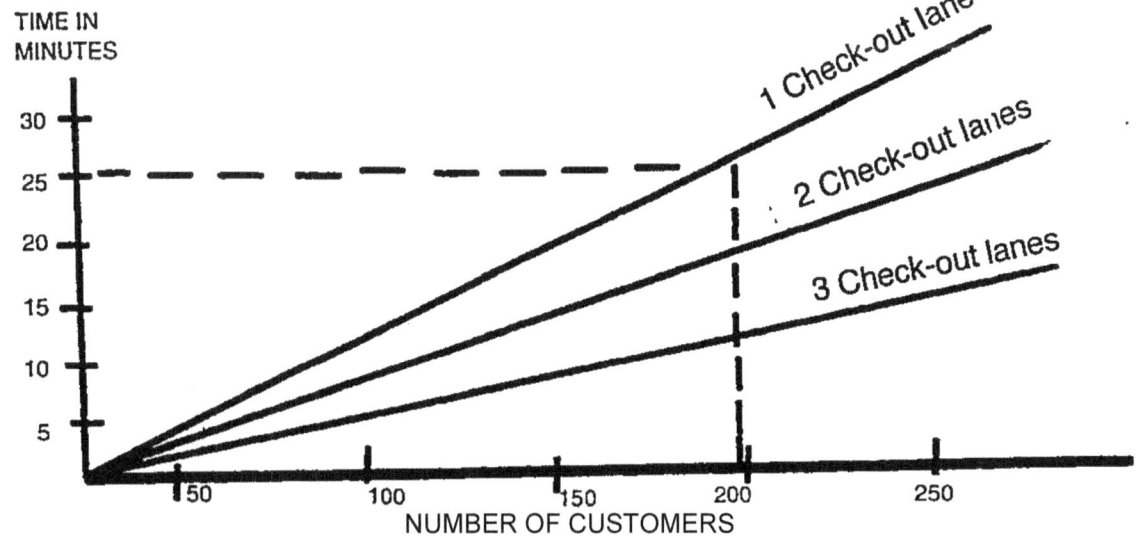

Note the dotted lines in Graph II. They demonstrate that, if there are 200 people in the store and only one check-out lane is open, the wait time will be 25 minutes.

1. At what time would a person be most likely NOT to have to wait more than 15 minutes if only one check-out lane is open?

    A. 11 A.M. B. 12 Noon C. 1 P.M. D. 3 P.M.

2. At what time of day would a person have to wait the LONGEST to check out if three check-out lanes are available?

    A. 11 A.M. B. 12 Noon C. 1 P.M. D. 2 P.M

3. The difference in wait times between 1 and 3 check-out lanes at 3 P.M. is MOST NEARLY

    A. 5 B. 10 C. 15 D. 20

TEST 4

DIRECTIONS: Each question or incomplete statement is followed by several suggested answers or completions. Select the one that BEST answers the question or completes the statement. *PRINT THE LETTER OF THE CORRECT ANSWER IN THE SPACE AT THE RIGHT.*

Questions 1-4.

DIRECTIONS: Questions 1 through 4 are to be answered SOLELY on the basis of the graph below.

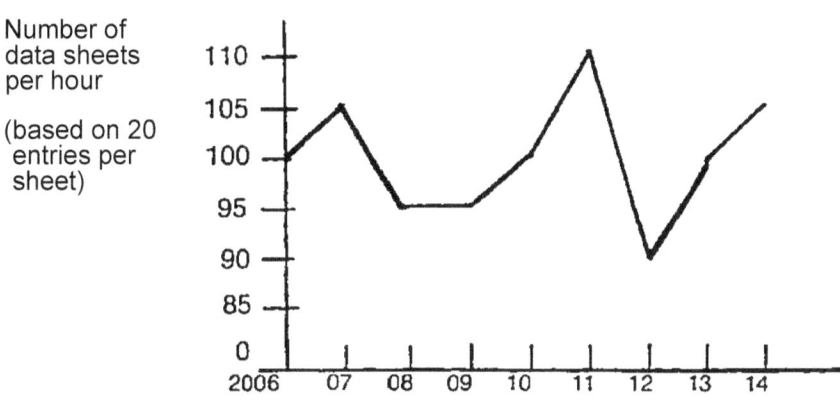

1. Of the following, during what four-year period did the average output of computer operators fall BELOW 100 sheets per hour?

    A. 2007-10   B. 2008-11   C. 2010-13   D. 2011-14

2. The average percentage change in output over the previous year's output for the years 2009 to 2012 is MOST NEARLY

    A. 2   B. 0   C. -5   D. -7

3. The difference between the actual output for 2012 and the projected figure based upon the average increase from 2006-2011 is MOST NEARLY

    A. 18   B. 20   C. 22   D. 24

4. Assume that after constructing the above graph you, an analyst, discovered that the average number of entries per sheet in 2012 was 25 (instead of 20) because of the complex nature of the work performed during that period.
The average output in sheets per hour for the period 2010-13, expressed in terms of 20 items per sheet, would then be MOST NEARLY

    A. 95   B. 100   C. 105   D. 110

TEST 6

DIRECTIONS: Each question or incomplete statement is followed by several suggested answers or completions. Select the one that BEST answers the question or completes the statement. *PRINT THE LETTER OF THE CORRECT ANSWER IN THE SPACE AT THE RIGHT.*

Questions 1-3.

DIRECTIONS: Questions 1 through 3 are to be answered on the basis of the following data assembled for a cost-benefit analysis.

	Cost	Benefit
No program	0	0
Alternative W	$ 3,000	$ 6,000
Alternative X	$10,000	$17,000
Alternative Y	$17,000	$25,000
Alternative Z	$30,000	$32,000

1. From the point of view of selecting the alternative with the best cost benefit ratio, the BEST alternative is Alternative

   A. W   B. X   C. Y   D. Z

2. From the point of view of selecting the alternative with the best measure of net benefit, the BEST alternative is Alternative

   A. W   B. X   C. Y   D. Z

3. From the point of view of pushing public expenditure to the point where marginal benefit equals or exceeds marginal cost, the BEST alternative is Alternative

   A. W   B. X   C. Y   D. Z

TEST 6

DIRECTIONS: Each question or incomplete statement is followed by several suggested answers or completions. Select the one that BEST answers the question or completes the statement. *PRINT THE LETTER OF THE CORRECT ANSWER IN THE SPACE AT THE RIGHT.*

Questions 1-3.

DIRECTIONS: Questions 1 through 3 are to be answered SOLELY on the basis of the following data.

A series of cost-benefit studies of various alternative health programs yields the following results:

Program	Benefit	Cost
K	30	15
L	60	60
M	300	150
N	600	500

In answering Questions 1 and 2, assume that all programs can be increased or decreased in scale without affecting their individual benefit-to-cost ratios.

1. The benefit-to-cost ratio of Program M is

   A. 10:1   B. 5:1   C. 2:1   D. 1:2

2. The budget ceiling for one or more of the programs included in the study is set at 75 units. It may MOST logically be concluded that

   A. Programs K and L should be chosen to fit within the budget ceiling
   B. Program K would be the most desirable one that could be afforded
   C. Program M should be chosen rather than Program K
   D. the choice should be between Programs M and K

3. If no assumptions can be made regarding the effects of change of scale, the MOST logical conclusion, on the basis of the data available, is that

   A. more data are needed for a budget choice of program
   B. Program K is the most preferable because of its low cost and good benefit-to-cost ratio
   C. Program M is the most preferable because of its high benefits and good benefit-to-cost ratio
   D. there is no difference between Programs K and M, and either can be chosen for any purpose

TEST 7

DIRECTIONS: Each question or incomplete statement is followed by several suggested answers or completions. Select the one that BEST answers the question or completes the statement. *PRINT THE LETTER OF THE CORRECT ANSWER IN THE SPACE AT THE RIGHT.*

Questions 1-6.

DIRECTIONS: Questions 1 through 6 are to be answered SOLELY on the basis of the information contained in the charts below which relate to the budget allocations of City X, a small suburban community. The charts depict the annual budget allocations by Department and by expenditures over a five-year period.

CITY X BUDGET IN MILLIONS OF DOLLARS
TABLE I. Budget Allocations by Department

Department	2017	2018	2019	2020	2021
Public Safety	30	45	50	40	50
Health and Welfare	50	75	90	60	70
Engineering	5	8	10	5	8
Human Resources	10	12	20	10	22
Conservation & Environment	10	15	20	20	15
Education & Development	15	25	35	15	15
TOTAL BUDGET	120	180	225	150	180

TABLE II. Budget Allocations by Expenditures

Category	2017	2018	2019	2020	2021
Raw Materials & Machinery	36	63	68	30	98
Capital Outlay	12	27	56	15	18
Personal Services	72	90	101	105	64
TOTAL BUDGET	120	180	225	150	180

1. The year in which the SMALLEST percentage of the total annual budget was allocated to the Department of Education and Development is

   A. 2017   B. 2018   C. 2020   D. 2021

2. Assume that in 2020 the Department of Conservation and Environment divided its annual budget into the three categories of expenditures and in exactly the same proportion as the budget shown in Table II for the year 2020. The amount allocated for capital outlay in the Department of Conservation and Environment's 2020 budget was MOST NEARLY _____ million.

   A. $2   B. $4   C. $6   D. $10

2 (#9)

3. From the year 2018 to the year 2020, the sum of the annual budgets for the Departments of Public Safety and Engineering showed an overall _____ million.

   A. decline; $8
   B. increase; $7
   C. decline; $15
   D. increase; $22

4. The LARGEST dollar increase in departmental budget allocations from one year to the next was in _____ from _____.

   A. Public Safety; 2017 to 2018
   B. Health and Welfare; 2017 to 2018
   C. Education and Development; 2019 to 2020
   D. Human Resources; 2019 to 2020

5. During the five-year period, the annual budget of the Department of Human Resources was GREATER than the annual budget for the Department of Conservation and Environment in _____ of the years.

   A. none   B. one   C. two   D. three

6. If the total City X budget increases at the same rate from 2021 to 2022 as it did from 2020 to 2021, the total City X budget for 2022 will be MOST NEARLY _____ million.

   A. $180   B. $200   C. $210   D. $215

TEST 8

DIRECTIONS: Each question or incomplete statement is followed by several suggested answers or completions. Select the one that BEST answers the question or completes the statement. *PRINT THE LETTER OF THE CORRECT ANSWER IN THE SPACE AT THE RIGHT.*

Questions 1-3.

DIRECTIONS: Questions 1 through 3 are to be answered SOLELY on the basis of the following information.

Assume that in order to encourage Program A, the State and Federal governments have agreed to make the following reimbursements for money spent on Program A, provided the unreimbursed balance is paid from City funds.

During Fiscal Year 2021-2022 - For the first $2 million expended, 50% Federal reimbursement and 30% State reimbursement; for the next $3 million, 40% Federal reimbursement and 20% State reimbursement; for the next $5 million, 20% Federal reimbursement and 10% State reimbursement. Above $10 million expended, no Federal or State reimbursement.

During Fiscal Year 2022-2023 - For the first $1 million expended, 30% Federal reimbursement and 20% State reimbursement; for the next $4 million, 15% Federal reimbursement and 10% State reimbursement. Above $5 million expended, no Federal or State reimbursement.

1. Assume that the Program A expenditures are such that the State reimbursement for Fiscal Year 2021-2022 will be $1 million.
   Then, the Federal reimbursement for Fiscal Year 2021-2022 will be

   A. $1,600,000   B. $1,800,000
   C. $2,000,000   D. $2,600,000

2. Assume that $8 million were to be spent on Program A in Fiscal Year 2022-2023.
   The TOTAL amount of unreimbursed City funds required would be

   A. $3,500,000   B. $4,500,000
   C. $5,500,000   D. $6,500,000

3. Assume that the City desires to have a combined total of $6 million spent in Program A during both the Fiscal Year 2021-2022 and the Fiscal Year 2022-2023.
   Of the following expenditure combinations, the one which results in the GREATEST reimbursement of City funds is _____ in Fiscal Year 2021-2022 and _____ in Fiscal Year 2022-2023.

   A. $5 million; $1 million   B. $4 million; $2 million
   C. $3 million; $3 million   D. $2 million; $4 million

KEY (CORRECT ANSWERS)

TEST 1

1. D
2. C
3. C

TEST 2

1. B
2. A
3. A
4. D

TEST 3

1. A
2. D
3. B

TEST 4

1. A
2. B
3. C
4. C

TEST 5

1. A
2. C
3. C

TEST 6

1. C
2. D
3. A

TEST 7

1. D
2. A
3. A
4. B
5. B
6. D

TEST 8

1. B
2. D
3. A

EXAMINATION SECTION

TEST 1

DIRECTIONS: Each question or incomplete statement is followed by several suggested answers or completions. Select the one that BEST answers the question or completes the statement. *PRINT THE LETTER OF THE CORRECT ANSWER IN THE SPACE AT THE RIGHT.*

1. Which one of the following generalizations is MOST likely to be INACCURATE and lead to judgmental errors in communication?
   A. A supervisor must be able to read with understanding.
   B. Misunderstanding may lead to dislike.
   C. Anyone can listen to another person and understand what he means.
   D. It is usually desirable to let a speaker talk until he is finished.

   1.____

2. Assume that, as a supervisor, you have been directed to inform your subordinates about the implementation of a new procedure which will affect their work.
   While communicating this information, you should do all of the following EXCEPT
   A. obtain the approval of your subordinates regarding the new procedure
   B. explain the reason for implementing the new procedure
   C. hold a staff meeting at a time convenient to most of your subordinates
   D. encourage a productive discussion of the new procedure

   2.____

3. Assume that you are in charge of a section that handles requests for information on matters received from the public. One day, you observe that a clerk under your supervision is using a method to log-in requests for information that is different from the one specified by you in the past. Upon questioning the clerk, you discover that instructions changing the old procedure were delivered orally by your supervisor on a day on which you were absent from the office.
   Of the following, the MOST appropriate action for you to take is to
   A. tell the clerk to revert to the old procedure at once
   B. ask your supervisor for information about the change
   C. call your staff together and tell them that no existing procedure is to be changed unless you direct that it be done
   D. write a memo to your supervisor suggesting that all future changes in procedure are to be in writing and that they be directed to you

   3.____

4. At the first meeting with your staff after appointment as a supervisor, you find considerable indifference and some hostility among the participants.
   Of the following, the MOST appropriate way to handle this situation is to
   A. disregard the attitudes displayed and continue to make your presentation until you have completed it
   B. discontinue your presentation but continue the meeting and attempt to find out the reasons for their attitudes

   4.____

C. warm up your audience with some good-natured statements and anecdotes and then proceed with your presentation
D. discontinue the meeting and set up personal interviews with the staff members to try to find out the reason for their attitude

5. In order to start the training of a new employee, it has been a standard practice to have him read a manual of instructions or procedures.
This method is currently being replaced by the _____ method.
   A. audio-visual
   B. conference
   C. lecture
   D. programmed instruction

5.____

6. Of the following subjects, the one that can usually be successfully taught by a first-line supervisor who is training his subordinates is:
   A. theory and philosophy of management
   B. human relations
   C. responsibilities of a supervisor
   D. job skills

6.____

7. Assume that as supervisor you are training a clerk who is experiencing difficulty learning a new task.
Which of the following would be the LEAST effective approach to take when trying to solve this problem? To
   A. ask questions which will reveal the clerk's understanding of the task
   B. take a different approach in explaining the task
   C. give the clerk an opportunity to ask questions about the task
   D. make sure the clerk knows you are watching his work closely

7.____

8. One school of management and supervision involves participation by employees in the setting of group goals and in the sharing of responsibility for the operation of the unit.
If this philosophy were applied to a unit consisting of professional and clerical personnel, one should expect
   A. the professional and clerical personnel to participate with equal effectiveness in operating areas and policy areas
   B. the professional personnel to participate with greater effectiveness than the clerical personnel in policy areas
   C. the clerical personnel to participate with greater effectiveness than the professional personnel in operating areas
   D. greater participation by clerical personnel but with less responsibility for their actions

8.____

9. With regard to productivity, high morale among employees generally indicates a
   A. history of high productivity
   B. nearly absolute positive correlation with high productivity
   C. predisposition to be productive under facilitating leadership and circumstances
   D. complacency which has little effect on productivity

9.____

10. Assume that you are going to organize the professionals and clerks under your supervision into work groups or team of two or three employees.
Of the following, the step which is LEAST likely to foster the successful development of each group is to

    A. allow friends to work together in the group
    B. provide special help and attention to employees with no friends in their group
    C. frequently switch employees from group to group
    D. rotate jobs within the group in order to strengthen group identification

10.____

11. Following are four statements which might be made by an employee to his supervisor during a performance evaluation interview.
Which of the statements BEST provides a basis for developing a plan to improve the employee's performance?

    A. *I understand that you are dissatisfied with my work and I will try harder in the future.*
    B. *I feel that I've been making too many careless clerical errors recently.*
    C. *I am aware that I will be subject to disciplinary action if my work does not improve within one month.*
    D. *I understand that this interview is simply a requirement of your job and not a personal attack on me.*

11.____

12. Three months ago, Mr. Smith and his supervisor, Mrs. Jones, developed a plan which was intended to correct Mr. Smith's inadequate job performance. Now, during a follow-up interview, Mr. Smith, who thought his performance had satisfactorily improved, has been informed that Mrs. Jones is still dissatisfied with his work.
Of the following, it is MOST likely that the disagreement occurred because, when formulating the plan, they did NOT

    A. set realistic goals for Mr. Smith's performance
    B. set a reasonable time limit for Mr. Smith to effect his improvement in performance
    C. provide for adequate training to improve Mr. Smith's skills
    D. establish performance standards for measuring Mr. Smith's progress

12.____

13. When a supervisor delegates authority to subordinates, there are usually many problems to overcome, such as inadequately trained subordinates and poor planning.
All of the following are means of increasing the effectiveness of delegation EXCEPT:

    A. Defining assignments in the light of results expected
    B. Maintaining open lines of communication
    C. Establishing tight controls so that subordinates will stay within the bounds of the area of delegation
    D. Providing rewards for successful assumption of authority by a subordinate

13.____

14. Assume that one of your subordinates has arrived late for work several times during the current month. The last time he was late you had warned him that another unexcused lateness would result informal disciplinary action.
If the employee arrives late for work again during this month, the FIRST action you should take is to
   A. give the employee a chance to explain this lateness
   B. give the employee a written copy of your warning
   C. tell the employee that you are recommending formal disciplinary action
   D. tell the employee that you will give him only one more chance before recommending formal disciplinary action

15. In trying to decide how many subordinates a manager can control directly, one of the determinants is how much the manager can reduce the frequency and time consumed in contacts with his subordinates.
Of the following, the factor which LEAST influences the number and direction of these contacts is:
   A. How well the manager delegates authority
   B. The rate at which the organization is changing
   C. The control techniques used by the manager
   D. Whether the activity is line or staff

16. Systematic rotation of employees through lateral transfer within a government organization to provide for managerial development is
   A. *good*, because systematic rotation develops specialists who learn to do many jobs well
   B. *bad*, because the outsider upsets the status quo of the existing organization
   C. *good*, because rotation provides challenge and organizational flexibility
   D. *bad*, because it is upsetting to employees to be transferred within a service

17. Assume that you are required to provide an evaluation of the performance of your subordinates.
Of the following factors, it is MOST important that the performance evaluation include a rating of each employee's
   A. initiative   B. productivity   C. intelligence   D. personality

18. When preparing performance evaluations of your subordinates, one way to help assure that you are rating each employee fairly is to
   A. prepare a list of all employees and all the rating factors and rate all employees on one rating factor before going on to the next factor
   B. prepare a list of all your employees and all the rating factors and rate each employee on all factors before going on to the next employee
   C. discuss all the ratings you anticipate giving with another supervisor in order to obtain an unbiased opinion
   D. discuss each employee with his co-workers in order to obtain peer judgment of worth before doing any rating

19. A managerial plan which would include the GREATEST control is a plan which is
    A. spontaneous and geared to each new job that is received
    B. detailed and covering an extended time period
    C. long-range and generalized, allowing for various interpretations
    D. specific and prepared daily

20. Assume that you are preparing a report which includes statistical data covering increases in budget allocations of four agencies for the past ten years.
    For you to represent the statistical data pictorially or graphically within the report is a
    A. *poor* idea, because you should be able to make statistical data understandable through the use of words
    B. *good* idea, because it is easier for the reader to understand pictorial representation rather than quantities of words conveying statistical data
    C. *poor* idea, because using pictorial representation in a report may make the report too expensive to print
    D. *good* idea, because a pictorial representation makes the report appear more attractive than the use of many words to convey the statistical data

KEY (CORRECT ANSWERS)

1.	C	11.	A
2.	A	12.	B
3.	B	13.	C
4.	D	14.	A
5.	D	15.	D
6.	D	16.	C
7.	D	17.	B
8.	B	18.	A
9.	C	19.	B
10.	C	20.	B

TEST 2

DIRECTIONS: Each question or incomplete statement is followed by several suggested answers or completions. Select the one that BEST answers the question or completes the statement. *PRINT THE LETTER OF THE CORRECT ANSWER IN THE SPACE AT THE RIGHT.*

1. Research studies have shown that supervisors of groups with high production records USUALLY
   A. give detailed instructions, constantly check on progress, and insist on approval of all decisions before implementation
   B. do considerable paperwork and other work similar to that performed by subordinates
   C. think of themselves as team members on the same level as others in the work group
   D. perform tasks traditionally associated with managerial functions

   1.____

2. Mr. Smith, a bureau chief, is summoned by his agency's head in a conference to discuss Mr. Jones, an accountant who works in one of the divisions of his bureau. Mr. Jones has committed an error of such magnitude as to arouse the agency head's concern.
   After agreeing with the other conferees that a severe reprimand would be the appropriate punishment, Mr. Smith SHOULD
   A. arrange for Mr. Jones to explain the reasons for his error to the agency head
   B. send a memorandum to Mr. Jones, being careful that the language emphasizes the nature of the error rather than Mr. Jones' personal faults
   C. inform Mr. Jones' immediate supervisor of the conclusion reached at the conference, and let the supervisor take the necessary action
   D. suggest to the agency head that no additional action be taken against Mr. Jones because no further damage will be caused by the error

   2.____

3. Assume that Ms. Thomson, a unit chief, has determined that the findings of an internal audit have been seriously distorted as a result of careless errors. The audit had been performed by a group of auditors in her unit and the errors were overlooked by the associate accountant in charge of the audit. Ms. Thomson has decided to delay discussing the matter with the associate accountant and the staff who performed the audit until she verifies certain details, which may require prolonged investigation.
   Mrs. Thomson's method of handling this situation is
   A. *appropriate*; employees should not be accused of wrongdoing until all the facts have been determined
   B. *inappropriate*; the employees involved may assume that the errors were considered unimportant
   C. *appropriate*; employees are more likely to change their behavior as a result of disciplinary action taken after a *cooling off* period
   D. *inappropriate*; the employees involved may have forgotten the details and become emotionally upset when confronted with the facts

   3.____

4. After studying the financial situation in his agency, an administrative accountant decides to recommend centralization of certain accounting functions which are being performed in three different bureaus of the organization
The one of the following which is MOST likely to be a DISADVANTAE if this recommendation is implemented is that
   A. there may be less coordination of the accounting procedure because central direction is not so close to the day-to-day problems as the personnel handling them in each specialized accounting unit
   B. the higher management levels would not be able to make emergency decisions in as timely a manner as the more involved, lower-level administrators who are closer to the problem
   C. it is more difficult to focus the attention of the top management in order to resolve accounting problems because of the many other activities top management is involved in at the same time
   D. the accuracy of upward and inter-unit communication may be reduced because centralization may require insertion of more levels of administration in the chain of command

5. Of the following assumptions about the role of conflict in an organization, the one which is the MOST accurate statement of the approach of modern management theorists is that conflict
   A. can usually be avoided or controlled
   B. serves as a vital element in organizational change
   C. works against attainment of organizational goals
   D. provides a constructive outlet for problem employees

6. Which of the following is generally regarded as the BEST approach for a supervisor to follow in handling grievances brought by subordinates?
   A. Avoid becoming involved personally
   B. Involve the union representative in the first stage of discussion
   C. Settle the grievance as soon as possible
   D. Arrange for arbitration by a third party

7. Assume that supervisors of similar-sized accounting units in city, state, and federal offices were interviewed and observed at their work. It was found that the ways they acted in and viewed their roles tended to be very similar, regardless of who employed them.
Which of the following is the BEST explanation of this similarity
   A. A supervisor will ordinarily behave in conformance to his own self-image.
   B. Each role in an organization, including the supervisory role, calls for a distinct type of personality.
   C. The supervisor role reflects an exceptionally complex pattern of human response.
   D. The general nature of the duties and responsibilities of the supervisory position determines the role.

8. Which of the following is NOT consistent with the findings of recent research about the characteristics of successful top managers?
   A. They are *inner-directed* and not overly concerned with pleasing others.
   B. They are challenged by situations filled with high risk and ambiguity.
   C. They tend to stay on the same job for long periods of time.
   D. They consider it more important to handle critical assignments successfully than to do routine work well.

9. As a supervisor, you have to give subordinates operational guidelines.
   Of the following, the BEST reason for providing them with information about the overall objectives within which their operations fit is that the subordinates will
   A. be more likely to carry out the operation according to your expectations
   B. know that there is a legitimate reason for carrying out the operation in the way you have prescribed
   C. be more likely to handle unanticipated problems that may arise without having to take up your time
   D. more likely to transmit the operating instructions correctly to their subordinates

10. A supervisor holds frequent meetings with his staff.
    Of the following, the BEST approach he can take in order to elicit productive discussions at these meetings is for him to
    A. ask questions of those who attend
    B. include several levels of supervisors at the meetings
    C. hold the meetings at a specified time each week
    D. begin each meeting with a statement that discussion is welcomed

11. Of the following, the MOST important action that a supervisor can take to increase the productivity of a subordinate is to
    A. increase his uninterrupted work time
    B. increase the number of reproducing machines available in the office
    C. provide clerical assistance whenever he requests it
    D. reduce the number of his assigned tasks

12. Assume that, as a supervisor, you find out that you often must countermand or modify your original staff memos.
    If this practice continues, which one of the following situations is MOST likely to occur? The
    A. staff will not bother to read your memos
    B. office files will become cluttered
    C. staff will delay acting on your memos
    D. memos will be treated routinely

13. In making management decisions, the committee approach is often used by managers.
    Of the following, the BEST reason for using this approach is to
    A. prevent any one individual from assuming too much authority
    B. allow the manager to bring a wider range of experience and judgment to bear on the problem

C. allow the participation of all staff members, which will make them feel more committed to the decisions reached
D. permit the rapid transmission of information about decisions reached to the staff members concerned

14. In establishing standards for the measurement of the performance of a management project team, it is MOST important for the project manager to
    A. identify and define the objectives of the project
    B. determine the number of people who will be assigned to the project team
    C. evaluate the skills of the staff who will be assigned to the project team
    D. estimate fairly accurately the length of time required to complete each phase of the project

14.____

15. It is virtually impossible to tell an employee either that he is not good as another employee or that he does not measure up to a desirable level of performance, without having him feel threatened, rejected, and discouraged.
In accordance with the foregoing observation, a supervisor who is concerned about the performance of the less efficient members of his staff should realize that
    A. he might obtain better results by not discussing the quality and quantity of their work with them, but by relying instead on the written evaluation of their performance to motivate their improvement
    B. since he is required to discuss their performance with them, he should do so in words of encouragement and in so friendly a manner as to not destroy their morale
    C. he might discuss their work in a general way, without mentioning any of the specifics about the quality of their performance, with the expectation that they would understand the full implications of his talk
    D. he should make it a point, while telling them of their poor performance, to mention that their work is as good as that of some of the other employees in the unit

15.____

16. Some advocates of management-by-objectives procedures in public agencies have been urging that this method of operations be expanded to encompass all agencies of the government, for one or more of the following reasons, not all of which may be correct:
    I. The MBO method is likely to succeed because it embraces the practice of setting near-term goals for the subordinate manager, reviewing accomplishments at an appropriate time, and repeating this process indefinitely
    II. Provision for authority to perform the tasks assigned as goals in the MBO method is normally not needed because targets are set in quantitative or qualitative terms and specific times for accomplishment are arranged in short-term, repetitive intervals
    III. Many other appraisal-of-performance programs failed because both supervisors and subordinates resisted them, while the MBO approach is not instituted until there is an organizational commitment to it
    IV. Personal accountability is clearly established through the MBO approach because verifiable results are set up in the process of formulating the targets

16.____

Which of the choices below includes ALL of the foregoing statements that are CORRECT?
A. I, III B. II, IV C. I, II, III, IV D. I, III, IV

17. In preparing an organizational structure, the PRINCIPAL guideline for locating staff units is to place them
    A. all under a common supervisor
    B. as close as possible to the activities they serve
    C. as close to the chief executive as possible without over-extending his span of control
    D. at the lowest operational level

17.____

18. The relative importance of any unit in a department can be LEAST reliably judged by the
    A. amount of office space allocated to the unit
    B. number of employees in the unit
    C. rank of the individual who heads the unit
    D. rank of the individual to whom the unit head reports directly

18.____

19. Those who favor Planning-Programming-Budgeting Systems (PPBS) as a new method of governmental financial administration emphasize that PPBS
    A. applies statistical measurements which correlate highly with criteria
    B. makes possible economic systems analysis, including an explicit examination of alternatives
    C. makes available scarce government resources which can be coordinated on a government-wide basis and shared between local units of government
    D. shifts the emphasis in budgeting methods to an automated system of data processing

19.____

20. The term applied to computer processing which processes data concurrently with a given activity and provides results soon enough to influence the selection of a course of action is _____ processing.
    A. realtime   B. batch
    C. random access   D. integrated data

20.____

KEY (CORRECT ANSWERS)

1.	D	11.	A
2.	C	12.	C
3.	B	13.	B
4.	D	14.	A
5.	B	15.	B
6.	C	16.	D
7.	D	17.	B
8.	C	18.	B
9.	C	19.	B
10.	A	20.	A

EXAMINATION SECTION

TEST 1

DIRECTIONS: Each question or incomplete statement is followed by several suggested answers or completions. Select the one that BEST answers the question or completes the statement. *PRINT THE LETTER OF THE CORRECT ANSWER IN THE SPACE AT THE RIGHT.*

1. When a supervisor in a large office introduces a change in the regular office procedure, it is USUAL to expect
   A. immediate acceptance by office staff, unless the change is unnecessary
   B. an immediate production increase, since new procedures are more stimulating than old ones
   C. a temporary production loss, even if the change is really an overall improvement
   D. resistance to the change only if it has been put into writing

   1._____

2. A supervisor evaluates the performance of subordinates and then applies measures, where needed, which result in bringing performance up to desired standards.
   Which of the following functions of management might he BEST be described as performing?
   A. Organizing   B. Controlling   C. Directing   D. Planning

   2._____

3. Assume that, as a supervisor, you have been assigned responsibility for a new and complex project which entails collection and analysis of data. You have prepared general written instructions which explain the project and procedures to be followed by several statisticians.
   Which of the following procedures would be MOST advisable for you, as the supervisor, to follow?
   A. Distribute the instructions to your subordinates to come to you with any important questions
   B. Distribute the instructions and advise subordinates to come to you with any important questions
   C. Meet with subordinates as a group and explain the project using the written instructions as a handout
   D. Delegate responsibility for further explanation of the project to an immediate qualified subordinate to free you for concentration on research design

   3._____

4. Supervisors have an obligation to make careful and thorough appraisals and reports of probationary employees.
   Of the following, the MOST important justification for this statement is that the probationary period
   A. should be used for positive development of the employee's understanding of the organization
   B. is the most effective period for changing a new employee's knowledges, skills, and attitudes

   4._____

2 (#1)

    C. insures that the employee will meet work standard requirements on future assignments
    D. should be considered as the final step in the selection process

5. Many studies of management indicate that a principal reason for failure of supervisors lies in their ability to delegate duties effectively.
   Which one of the following practices by a supervisor would NOT be a block to successful delegation?
   A. Instructing the delegate to follow a set procedure in carrying out the assignment
   B. Maintaining point-by-point control over the process delegated
   C. Transferring ultimate responsibility for the duties assigned to the delegate
   D. Requiring the delegate to keep the delegator informed of his progress

5._____

6. Crosswise communication occurs between personnel at lower or middle levels of different organizational units. It often speeds information and improves understanding, but has certain dangers.
   Of the following proposed policies, which would NOT be important as a safeguard in crosswise communication?
   A. Supervisors should agree as to how crosswise communication should occur.
   B. Crosswise relationships must exist only between employees of equal status.
   C. Subordinates must keep their superiors informed about their interdepartmental communications.
   D. Subordinates must refrain from making commitments beyond their authority.

6._____

7. Systems theory has given us certain principles which are as applicable to organizational and social activities as they are to those of science.
   With regard to the training of employees in an organization, which of the following is likely to be MOST consistent with the modern systems approach?
   Training can be effective ONLY when it is
   A. related to the individual abilities of the employees
   B. done on all levels of the organizational hierarchy
   C. evaluated on the basis of experimental and control groups
   D. provided on the job by the immediate supervisor

7._____

8. The management of a large agency, before making a decision as to whether or not to computerize its operations, should have a feasibility study made.
   Of the following, the one which is LEAST important to include in such a study is
   A. the current abilities of management and staff to use a computer
   B. projected workloads and changes in objectives of functional units in the agency
   C. the contributions expected of each organizational unit towards achievement of agency objectives
   D. the decision-making activity and informational needs of each management function

8._____

9. Managing information covers the creation, collection, processing, storage, and transmission of information that appears in a variety of forms. A supervisor responsible for a statistical unit can be considered, in many respects, an information manager.
Of the following, which would be considered the LEAST important aspect of the information manager's job?
   A. Establishing better information standards and forms
   B. Reducing the amount of unnecessary paperwork performed
   C. Producing progressively greater numbers of informational reports
   D. Developing a greater appreciation for information among management members

10. Because of the need for improvement in information systems throughout industry and government, various techniques for improving these systems have been developed.
Of these, *systems simulation* is a technique for improving systems which
   A. creates new ideas and concepts through the use of a computer
   B. deals with time controlling of interrelated systems which make up an overall project
   C. permits experimentation with various ideas to see what results might be obtained
   D. does not rely on assumptions which condition the value of the results

11. The one of the following which it is NOT advisable for a supervisor to do when dealing with individual employees is to
   A. recognize a person's outstanding service as well as his mistakes
   B. help an employee satisfy his need to excel
   C. encourage an efficient employee to seek better opportunities even if this action may cause the supervisor to lose a good worker
   D. take public notice of an employee's mistakes so that fewer errors will be made in the future

12. Suppose that you are in a department where you are given the responsibility for teaching seven new assistants a number of routine procedures that all assistants should know.
Of the following, the BEST method for you to follow in teaching these procedures is to
   A. separate the slower learners from the faster learners and adapt your presentation to their level of ability
   B. instruct all the new employees in a group without attempting to assess differences in learning rates
   C. restrict your approach to giving them detailed written instructions in order to save time
   D. avoid giving the employees written instructions in order to force them to memorize job procedures quickly

13. Suppose that you are a supervisor to whom several assistants must hand in work for review. You notice that one of the assistants gets very upset whenever you discover an error in his work, although all the assistants make mistakes from time to time.
Of the following, it would be BEST for you to
    A. arrange discreetly for the employee's work to be reviewed by another supervisor
    B. ignore his reaction since giving attention to such behavior increases its intensity
    C. suggest that the employee seek medical help since he has such great difficulty in accepting normal criticism
    D. try to build the employee's self-confidence by emphasizing those parts of his work that are done well

14. Suppose you are a supervisor responsible for supervising a number of assistants in an agency where each assistant receives a manual of policies and procedures when he first reports for work. You have been asked to teach your subordinates a new procedure which requires knowledge of several items of policy and procedure found in the manual.
The one of the following techniques which it would be BEST for you to employ is to
    A. give verbal instructions which include a review of the appropriate standard procedures as well as an explanation of new tasks
    B. give individual instruction restricted to the new procedure to each assistant as the need arises
    C. provide written instructions for new procedural elements and refer employees to their manuals for explanation of standard procedures
    D. ask employees to review appropriate sections of their manual and then explain those aspects of the new procedure which the manual did not cover

15. Supposes that you are a supervisor in charge of a unit in which changes in work procedures are about to be instituted.
The one of the following which you, as the supervisor, should anticipate as being MOST likely to occur during the changeover is
    A. a temporary rise in production because of interest in the new procedures
    B. uniform acceptance of these procedures on the part of your staff
    C. varying interpretations of the new procedures by your staff
    D. general agreement among staff members that the new procedures are advantageous

16. Suppose that a supervisor and one of the assistants under his supervision are known to be friends who play golf together on weekends.
The maintenance of such a friendship on the part of the supervisor is GENERALLY
    A. *acceptable* as long as this assistant continues to perform his duties satisfactorily
    B. *unacceptable* since the supervisor will find it difficult to treat the assistant as a subordinate

C. *acceptable* if the supervisor does not favor this assistant above other employees
D. *unacceptable* because the other assistants will resent the friendship regardless of the supervisor's behavior on the job

17. Suppose that you are a supervisor assigned to review the financial records of an agency which has recently undergone a major reorganization.
Which of the following would it be BEST for you to do FIRST?
    A. Interview the individual in charge of agency financial operations to determine whether the organizational changes affect the system of financial review
    B. Discuss the nature of the reorganization with your own supervisor to anticipate and plan a new financial review procedure
    C. Carry out the financial review as usual, and adjust your methods to any problems arising from the reorganization
    D. Request a written report from the agency head explaining the nature of the reorganization and recommending changes in the system of financial review

17.____

18. Suppose that a newly assigned supervisor finds that he must delegate some of his duties to subordinates in order to get the work done.
Which one of the following would NOT be a block to his delegating these duties effectively?
    A. Inability to give proper directions as to what he wants done
    B. Reluctance to take calculated risks
    C. Lack of trust in his subordinates
    D. Retaining ultimate responsibility for the delegated work

18.____

19. A supervisor sometimes performs the staff function of preparing and circulating reports among bureau chiefs.
Which of the following is LEAST important as an objective in designing and writing such reports?
    A. Providing relevant information on past, present, and future actions
    B. Modifying his language in order to insure goodwill among the bureau chiefs
    C. Helping the readers of the report to make appropriate decisions
    D. Summarizing important information to help readers see trends or outstanding points

19.____

20. Suppose you are a supervisor assigned to prepare a report to be read by all bureau chiefs in your agency.
The MOST important reason for avoiding highly technical accounting terminology in writing this report is to
    A. ensure the accuracy and relevancy of the text
    B. insure winning the readers' cooperation
    C. make the report more interesting to the readers
    D. make it easier for the readers to understand

20.____

21. Which of the following conditions is MOST likely to cause low morale in an office?
    A. Different standards of performance for individuals in the same title
    B. A requirement that employees perform at full capacity
    C. Standards of performance that vary with titles of employees
    D. Careful attention to the image of the division or department

22. A wise supervisor or representative of management realizes that, in the relationship between supervisor and subordinates, all power is not on the side of management, and that subordinates do sometimes react to restrictive authority in such a manner as to seriously retard management's objectives. A wise supervisor does not stimulate such reactions.
    In the subordinate's attempt to retaliate against an unusually authoritative management style, which of the following actions would generally be LEAST successful for the subordinate? He
    A. joins with other employees in organizations to deal with management
    B. obviously delays in carrying out instructions which are given in an arrogant or incisive manner
    C. performs assignments exactly as instructed even when he recognizes errors in instructions
    D. holds back the flow of feedback information to superiors

23. Which of the following is the MOST likely and costly effect of vague and indefinite instructions given to subordinates by a supervisor?
    A. Misunderstanding and ineffective work on the part of the subordinates
    B. A necessity for the supervisor to report identical instructions with each assignment
    C. A failure of the supervisor to adequately keep the attention of subordinates
    D. Inability of subordinates to assist each other in the absence of the supervisor

24. At the professional level, there is a kind of informal authority which exercises itself even though no delegation of authority has taken place from higher management. It occurs within the context of knowledge required and professional competence in a special area.
    An example of the kind of authority described in this statement is MOST clearly exemplified in the situation where a senior supervisor influences associates and subordinates by virtue of the
    A. salary level fixed for his particular set of duties
    B. amount of college training he possesses
    C. technical position he has gained and holds on the work team
    D. initiative and judgment he has demonstrated to his supervisor

25. An assistant under your supervision attempts to conceal the fact that he has made an error.
    Under this circumstance, it would be BEST for you, as the supervisor, to proceed on the assumption that

A. this evasion indicates something wrong in the fundamental relationship between you and the assistant
B. this evasion is not deliberate, if the error is subsequently corrected by the assistant
C. this evasion should be overlooked if the error is not significant
D. detection and correction of errors will come about as an automatic consequence of internal control procedures

KEY (CORRECT ANSWERS)

1.	C	11.	D
2.	B	12.	B
3.	C	13.	D
4.	D	14.	A
5.	D	15.	C
6.	B	16.	C
7.	B	17.	A
8.	A	18.	D
9.	C	19.	B
10.	C	20.	D

21.	A
22.	B
23.	A
24.	C
25.	A

TEST 2

DIRECTIONS: Each question or incomplete statement is followed by several suggested answers or completions. Select the one that BEST answers the question or completes the statement. *PRINT THE LETTER OF THE CORRECT ANSWER IN THE SPACE AT THE RIGHT.*

1. The unit which you supervise has a number of attorneys, accountants, examiners, statisticians, and clerks who prepare some of the routine papers required to be filed. In order to be certain that nothing goes out of your office that is improper, you have instituted a system that requires that you review and initial all moving papers, memoranda of law and briefs that are prepared. As a result, you put in a great deal of overtime and even must take work home with you frequently.
A situation such as this is
   A. inevitable if you are to keep proper controls over the quality of the office work product
   B. indicative of the fact that the agency must provide an additional position within your office for an assistant supervisor who would do all the reviewing, leaving you free for other pressing administrative work and to handle the most difficult work in your unit
   C. the logical result of an ever-increasing caseload
   D. symptomatic of poor supervision and management

1.____

2. Your unit has been assigned a new employee who has never worked for the city.
To orient him to his job in your unit, of the following, the BEST procedure is first to
   A. assign him to another employee to whatever work that employee gives him so that he can become familiar with your work and at the same time be productive
   B. give him copies of the charter and code provisions affecting your operations plus any in-office memoranda or instructions that are available and have him read them
   C. assign him to work on a relatively simple problem and then, after he has finished it, tell him politely what he did wrong
   D. explain to him the duties of his position and the functions of the office

2.____

3. A bureau chief who supervises other supervisors makes it a practice to assign them more cases than they can possibly handle.
This approach is
   A. *right*, because it results in getting more work done than would otherwise be the case
   B. *right*, because it relieves the bureau chief making the assignments of the responsibility of getting the work done
   C. *wrong*, because it builds resistance on the part of those called upon to handle the caseload
   D. *wrong*, because superiors lose track of cases

3.____

4. Assume you are a supervisor and are expected to exercise *authority* over subordinates.
   Which of the following BEST defines *authority*? The
   A. ability to control the nature of the contribution a subordinate is desirous of making
   B. innate inability to get others to do for you what you want to get done irrespective of their own wishes
   C. legal right conferred by the agency to control the actions of others
   D. power to determine a subordinate's attitude toward his agency and his superiors

5. Paternalistic leadership stresses a paternal or fatherly influence in the relationships between the leader and the group and is manifest in a watchful care for the comfort and welfare of the followers.
   Which one of the following statements regarding paternalistic leadership is MOST accurate?
   A. Employees who work well under paternalistic leadership come to expect such leadership even when the paternal leader has left the organization.
   B. Most disputes arising out of supervisor-subordinate relationships develop because group leaders do not understand the principles of paternalistic leadership.
   C. Paternalistic leadership frequently destroys office relationships because most employees are turned into non-thinking dependent robots.
   D. Paternalistic leadership is rarely, if ever, successful because employees resent paternalistic leadership which they equate with weakness.

6. Employees who have extensive dealings with members of the public should have, as much as possible, *real acceptance* of all people and a willingness to serve everyone impartially and objectively.
   Assuming that this statement is correct, the one of the following which would be the BEST demonstration of *real acceptance* is
   A. condoning antisocial behavior
   B. giving the appearance of agreeing with everyone encountered
   C. refusing to give opinions on anyone's behavior
   D. understanding the feelings expressed through a person's behavior

7. Assume that the agency chief has requested you to help plan a public relations program because of recent complaints from citizens about the unbecoming conduct and language of various groups of city employees who have dealings with the public.
   In carrying out this assignment, the one of the following steps which should be undertaken FIRST is to
   A. study the characteristics of the public clientele dealt with by employees in your agency
   B. arrange to have employees attend several seminars on human relations
   C. develop several procedures for dealing with the public and allow the staff to choose the one which is best
   D. find out whether the employees in your agency may oppose any plan proposed by you

8. The one of the following statements which BEST expresses the relationship between the morale of government employees and the public relations aspects of their work is:
   A. There is little relationship between employee morale and public relations, chiefly because public opinion is shaped primarily by response to departmental policy formulation.
   B. Employee morale is closely related to public relations, chiefly because the employee's morale will largely determine the manner in which he deals with the public.
   C. There is little relationship between employee morale and public relations, chiefly because public relations is primarily a function of the agency's public relations department.
   D. Employee morale is closely related to public relations, chiefly because employee morale indicates the attitude of the agency's top officials toward the public.

9. As a supervisor, you are required to deal extensively with the public. The agency chief has indicated that he is considering holding a special in-service training course for employees in communications skills
   Holding this training course would be
   A. *advisable*, chiefly because government employees should receive formal training in public relations skills
   B. *inadvisable*, chiefly because the public regards such training as a *waste of the taxpayers money*
   C. *advisable*, chiefly because such training will enable the employee to aid in drafting departmental press releases
   D. *inadvisable*, chiefly because of the great difficulty involved in developing skills through formal instruction

10. Assume that you have extensive contact with the public. In dealing with the public, sensitivity to an individual's attitudes is important because these attitudes can be used to predict behavior.
    However, the MAIN reason that attitudes CANNOT successfully predict all behavior is that
    A. attitudes are highly resistant to change
    B. an individual acquires attitudes as a function of growing up in a particular cultural environment
    C. attitudes are only one of many factors which determine a person's behavior
    D. an individual's behavior is not always observable

11. Rotation of employees from assignment to assignment is sometimes advocated by management experts.
    Of the following, the MOST probable advantage to the organization of this practice is that it leads to
    A. higher specialization of duties so that excessive identification with the overall organization is reduced
    B. increased loyalty of employees to their immediate supervisors

C. greater training and development of employees
D. intensified desire of employees to obtain additional, outside formal education

12. Usually, a supervisor should attempt to standardize the work for which he is responsible.
The one of the following which is a BASIC reason for doing this is to
    A. eliminate the need to establish priorities
    B. permit the granting of exceptions to rules and special circumstances
    C. facilitate the taking of action based on applicable standards
    D. learn the identity of outstanding employees

13. The differences between line and staff authority are often quite ambiguous. Of the following, the ESSENTIAL difference is that
    A. *line authority* is exercised by first-level supervisors; *staff authority* is exercised by higher-level supervisors and managerial staff
    B. *staff authority* is the right to issue directives; *line authority* is entirely consultative
    C. *line authority* is the power to make decisions regarding intra-agency matters; *staff authority* involves decisions regarding inter-agency matters
    D. *staff authority* is largely advisory; *line authority* is the right to command

14. Modern management theory stresses work-centered motivation as one way of increasing the productivity of employees.
The one of the following which is PARTICULARLY characteristic of such motivation is that it
    A. emphasizes the crucial role of routinization of procedures
    B. stresses the satisfaction to be found in performing work
    C. features the value of wages and fringe benefits
    D. uses a firm but fair method of discipline

15. The agency's informal communications network is called the *grapevine*. If employees are learning about important organizational developments primarily through the grapevine, this is MOST likely an indication that
    A. official channels of communication are not functioning so efficiently as they should
    B. supervisory personnel are making effective use of the grapevine to communicate with subordinates
    C. employees already have a clear understanding of the agency's policies and procedures
    D. upward formal channels of communication within the agency are informing management of employee grievances

16. Of the following, a flow chart is BEST described as a chart which shows
    A. the places through which work moves in the course of the job process
    B. which employees perform specific functions leading to the completion of a job

C. the schedules for production and how they eliminate waiting time between jobs
D. how work units are affected by the actions of related work units

17. Evaluation of the results of training is necessary in order to assess its value. Of the following, the BEST technique for the supervisor to use in determining whether the training under consideration actually resulted in the desired modification of the behavior of the employee concerned is through
    A. inference   B. job analysis   C. observation   D. simulation

17._____

18. The usual distinction between line and staff authority is that staff authority is mainly advisory, whereas line authority is the right to command. However, a third category has been suggested-prescriptive-to distinguish those personnel whose functions may be formally defined as staff but in practice exercise considerable authority regarding decisions relating to their specialties.
    The one of the following which indicates the MAJOR purpose of creating this third category is to
    A. develop the ability of each employee to perform a greater number of tasks
    B. reduce line-staff conflict
    C. prevent over-specialization of functions
    D. encourage decision-making by line personnel

18._____

19. It is sometimes considered desirable to train employees to a standard of proficiency higher than that deemed necessary for actual job performance. The MOST likely reason for such overtraining would be to
    A. eliminate the need for standards
    B. increase the value of refresher training
    C. compensate for previous lack of training
    D. reduce forgetting or loss of skill

19._____

20. Assume that you have been directed to immediately institute various new procedures in the handling of records.
    Of the following, the BEST method for you to use to insure that your subordinates know exactly what to do is to
    A. circulate a memorandum explaining the new procedure have your subordinates initial it
    B. explain the new procedures to one or two subordinates and ask them to tell the others
    C. have a meeting with your subordinates to give them copies of the procedures and discuss it with them
    D. post the new procedures where they can be referred to by all those concerned

20._____

21. A supervisor decided to hold a problem-solving conference with his entire staff and distributed an announcement and agenda one week before the meeting.
    Of the following, the BEST reason for providing each participant with an agenda is that
    A. participants will feel that something will be accomplished
    B. participants may prepare for the conference
    C. controversy will be reduced
    D. the top man should state the expected conclusions

22. In attempting to motivate employees, rewards are considered preferable to punishment PRIMARILY because
    A. punishment seldom has any effect on human behavior
    B. punishment usually results in decreased production
    C. supervisors find it difficult to punish
    D. rewards are more likely to result in willing cooperation

23. In an attempt to combat the low morale in his organization, a high-level supervisor publicized an *open-door* policy to allow employees who wished to do so to come to him with their complaints.
    Which of the following is LEAST likely to account for the fact that no employee came in with a complaint?
    A. Employees are generally reluctant to go over the heads of their immediate supervisors.
    B. The employees did not feel that management would help them.
    C. The low morale was not due to complaints association with the job
    D. The employees felt that they had more to lose than to gain.

24. It is MOST desirable to use written instructions rather than oral instructions for a particular job when
    A. a mistake on the job will not be serious
    B. the job can be completed in a short time
    C. there is no need to explain the job minutely
    D. the job involves many details

25. You have been asked to prepare for public distribution a statement dealing with a controversial matter.
    Of the following approaches, the one which would usually be MOST effective is to present your department's point of view
    A. as tersely as possible with no reference to any other matters
    B. developed from ideas and facts well known to most readers
    C. and show all the statistical data and techniques which were used in arriving at it
    D. in such a way that the controversial parts are omitted

KEY (CORRECT ANSWERS)

1.	D	11.	C
2.	D	12.	C
3.	C	13.	D
4.	C	14.	B
5.	A	15.	A
6.	D	16.	A
7.	A	17.	C
8.	B	18.	B
9.	A	19.	D
10.	C	20.	C

21.	B
22.	D
23.	C
24.	D
25.	B

TEST 3

DIRECTIONS: Each question or incomplete statement is followed by several suggested answers or completions. Select the one that BEST answers the question or completes the statement. *PRINT THE LETTER OF THE CORRECT ANSWER IN THE SPACE AT THE RIGHT.*

1. An administrator who supervises other supervisors makes it a practice to set deadline dates for completion of assignments.
   A NATURAL consequence of setting deadline dates is that
   A. supervisors will usually wait until the deadline date before they give projects their wholehearted attention
   B. projects are completed sooner than if no deadline dates are set
   C. such dates are ignored even though they are conspicuously posted
   D. the frequency of errors sharply increases resulting in an inability to meet deadlines

   1.____

2. Assume that you are chairing a meeting of the members of your staff. You throw out a question to the group. No one answers your question immediately, so that you find yourself faced with silence.
   In the circumstances, it would probably be BEST for you to
   A. ask the member of the group who appears to be least attentive to repeat the question
   B. change the topic quickly
   C. repeat the question carefully, pronouncing each word, and if there is still no response, repeat the question an additional time
   D. wait for an answer since someone will usually say something to break the tension

   2.____

3. Assume that you are holding a meeting with the members of your staff. John, a member of the unit, keeps sidetracking the subject of the discussion by bringing up extraneous matters. You deal with the situation by saying to him after he has raised an immaterial point, *"That's an interesting point John, but can you show me how it ties in with what we're talking about?"*
   Your approach in this situation would GENERALLY be considered
   A. *bad*; you have prevented the group from discussing not only extraneous matters but pertinent material as well
   B. *bad*; you have seriously humiliated John in front of the entire group
   C. *good*; you have pointed out how the discussion is straying from the main topic
   D. *good*; you have prevented John from presenting extraneous matters at future meetings

   3.____

4. Assume that a senior supervisor is asked to supervise a group of staff personnel. The work of one of these staff men meets minimum standards of acceptability. However, this staff man constantly looks for something at which to take offense. In any conversation with either a fellow staff man or with a superior, he views the slightest criticism as a grave insult.

   4.____

In this case, the senior supervisor should
- A. advise the staff man that the next time he refuses to accept criticism, he will be severely reprimanded
- B. ask member of the group for advice on how to deal with this staff man
- C. make it a practice to speak calmly, slowly, and deliberately to this staff man and question him frequently to make sure that there is no breakdown in communications
- D. recognize that professional help may be required and that this problem may not be conducive to a solution by a supervisor

5. Assume that you discover that one of the staff in preparing certain papers has made a serious mistake which has become obvious.
   In dealing with this situation, it would be BEST for you to begin by
   - A. asking the employee how the mistake happened
   - B. asking the employee to read through the papers to see whether he can correct the mistake
   - C. pointing out to the employee that, while an occasional error is permissible, frequent errors can prove a source of embarrassment to all concerned
   - D. pointing to the mistake and asking the employee whether he realizes the consequences of the mistake

5.____

6. You desire to develop teamwork among the members of your staff. You are assigned a case which will require that two of the staff work together if the papers are to be prepared in time. You decided to assign two employees, whom you know to be close friends, to work on these papers.
   Your action in this regard would GENERALLY be considered
   - A. *bad*; friends working together tend to do as little as they can get away with
   - B. *bad*; people who are friends socially often find that the bonds of friendship disintegrate in work situations
   - C. *good*; friends who are permitted to work together show their appreciation by utilizing every opportunity to reinforce the group leader's position of authority
   - D. *good*; the evidence suggests that more work can be done in this way

6.____

7. You notice that all of the employees, without exception, take lunch hours which in your view are excessively long. You call each of them to your desk and point out that unless this practice is brought to a stop, appropriate action will be taken.
   The way in which you handled this problem would GENERALLY be considered
   - A. *proper*, primarily because a civil servant, no matter what his professional status, owes the public a full day's work for a full day's pay
   - B. *proper*, primarily because employees need to have a clear picture of the rewards and penalties that go with public employment
   - C. *improper*, primarily because group problems require group discussion which need not be formal in character
   - D. *improper*, primarily because professional personnel resent having such matters as lunch hours brought to their attention

7.____

8. In communicating with superiors or subordinates, it is well to bear in mind a phenomenon known as the *halo effect*. An example of this *halo effect* occurs when we
   A. employ informal language in a formal setting as a means of attracting attention
   B. ignore the advice of someone we distrust without evaluating the advice
   C. ask people to speak up who have a tendency to speak softly or occasionally indistinctly
   D. react to a piece of good work by inquiring into the motivations of those who did the work

8.____

9. Which of the following dangers is MOST likely to arise when a work group becomes too tightly knit? The
   A. group may appoint an informal leader who gradually sets policies and standards for the group to the detriment of the agency
   B. group may be reluctant to accept new employees as members
   C. quantity and quality of work produced may tend to diminish sharply despite the group's best efforts
   D. group may focus too strongly on employee benefits at inappropriate times

9.____

10. The overall managerial problem has become more complex because each group of management specialists will tend to view the interests of the enterprise in terms which are compatible with the survival or the increase of its special function. That is, each group will have a trained capacity for its own function and a *trained incapacity* to see its relation to the whole.
    The *trained incapacity* to which the foregoing passage refers PROBABLY results from
    A. an imbalance in the number of specialists as compared with the number of generalists
    B. development by each specialized group of a certain dominant value or goal that shapes its entire way of doing things
    C. low morale accompanied by lackadaisical behavior by large segments of the managerial staff
    D. supervisory failure to inculcate pride in workmanship

10.____

11. Of the following, the MOST important responsibility of a supervisor in charge of a section is to
    A establish close personal relationships with each of his subordinates in the section
    B. insure that each subordinate in the section knows the full range of his duties and responsibilities
    C. maintain friendly relations with his immediate supervisor
    D. protect his subordinates from criticism from any source

11.____

12. The BEST way to get a good work output from employees is to
    A. hold over them the threat of disciplinary action or removal
    B. maintain a steady, unrelenting pressure on them
    C. show them that you can do anything they can do faster and better
    D win their respect and liking so they want to work for you

12.____

13. Supervisors should GENERALLY
    A. lean more toward management than toward their subordinates
    B. lean neither toward subordinates nor management
    C. lean more toward their subordinates than toward their management
    D. maintain a proper balance between management and subordinates

14. For a supervisor in charge of a section to ask occasionally the opinion of a subordinate concerning a problem is
    A. *desirable*; but it would be even better if the subordinate were consulted routinely on every problem
    B. *desirable*; subordinates may make good suggestions and will be pleased by being consulted
    C. *undesirable*; subordinates may be resentful if their advice is not followed
    D. *undesirable*; the supervisor should not attempt to shift his responsibilities to subordinates

15. The PRIMARY responsibility of a supervisor is to
    A. gain the confidence and make friends of all his subordinates
    B. get the work done properly
    C. satisfy his superior and gain his respect
    D. train the men in new methods for doing the work

16. In starting a work simplification study, the one of the following steps that should be taken FIRST is to
    A. break the work down into its elements
    B. draw up a chart of operations
    C. enlist the interest and cooperation of the personnel
    D. suggest alternative procedures

17. Of the following, the MOST important value of a manual of procedures is that it usually
    A. eliminates the need for on-the-job training
    B. decreases the span of control which can be exercised by individual supervisory personnel
    C. outlines methods of operation for ready reference
    D. provides concrete examples of work previously performed by employees

18. Reprimanding a subordinate when he has done something wrong should be done PRIMARILY in order to
    A. deter others from similar acts
    B. improve the subordinate in future performance
    C. maintain discipline
    D. uphold departmental rules

19. Most of the training of new employees in a public agency is USUALLY accomplished by
    A. formal classes
    B. general orientation
    C. internship
    D. on-the-job activities

20. You find that delivery of a certain item cannot possibly be made to a using agency by the date the using agency requested.
    Of the following, the MOST advisable course of action for you to take FIRST is to
    A. cancel the order and inform the using agency
    B. discuss the problem with the using agency
    C. notify the using agency to obtain the item through direct purchase
    D. schedule the delivery for the earliest possible date

21. Assume that one of your subordinates has gotten into the habit of regularly and routinely referring every small problem which arises in his work to you.
    In order to help him overcome this habit, it is generally MOST advisable for you to
    A. advise him that you do not have time to discuss each problem with him and that he should do whatever he wants
    B. ask your subordinate for his solution and approve any satisfactory approach that he suggests
    C. refuse to discuss such routine problems with him
    D. tell him that he should consider looking for another position if he does not feel competent to solve such routine problems

22. The BEST of the following reasons for developing understudies to supervisory staff is that this practice
    A. assures that capable staff will not leave their jobs since they are certain to be promoted
    B. helps to assure continued efficiency when persons in important positions leave their jobs
    C. improves morale by demonstrating to employees the opportunities for advancement
    D. provides an opportunity for giving on-the-job training

23. When a supervisor delegates some of his work to a subordinate, the
    A. supervisor retains final responsibility for the work
    B. supervisor should not check on the work until it has been completed
    C. subordinate assumes full responsibility for the successful completion of the work
    D. subordinate is likely to lose interest and get less satisfaction from the work

24. Sometimes it is necessary to give out written orders or to post written or typed information on a bulletin board rather than to merely give spoken orders. The supervisor must decide how he will do it.
    In which of the following situations would it be BETTER for him to give written rather than spoken orders?
    A. He is going to reassign a man from one unit to another under his supervision.
    B. His staff must be informed of a permanent change in a complicated operating procedure.

C. A man must be transferred from a clerical unit to an operating unit.
D. He must order a group of staff men to do a difficult and tedious inventory job to which most of them are likely to object.

25. Of the following symbolic patterns, which one is NOT representative of a normal direction in which formal organizational communications flow?

A. I B. II C. III D. IV

KEY (CORRECT ANSWERS)

1. B
2. D
3. C
4. D
5. A

6. D
7. C
8. B
9. B
10. B

11. B
12. D
13. D
14. B
15. B

16. C
17. C
18. B
19. D
20. B

21. B
22. B
23. A
24. B
25. B

REPORT WRITING

EXAMINATION SECTION

TEST 1

DIRECTIONS: Each question or incomplete statement is followed by several suggested answers or completions. Select the one that BEST answers the question or completes the statement. *PRINT THE LETTER OF THE CORRECT ANSWER IN THE SPACE AT THE RIGHT.*

Questions 1-4.

DIRECTIONS: Answer Questions 1 through 4 on the basis of the following report which was prepared by a supervisor for inclusion in his agency's annual report.

Line #
1 On Oct. 13, I was assigned to study the salaries paid.
2 to clerical employees in various titles by the city and by
3 private industry in the area.
4 In order to get the data I needed, I called Mr. Johnson at
5 the Bureau of the Budget and the payroll officers at X Corp.—
6 a brokerage house, Y Co. —an insurance company, and Z Inc. —
7 a publishing firm. None of them was available and I had to call
8 all of them again the next day.
9 When I finally got the information I needed, I drew up a
10 chart, which is attached. Note that not all of the companies I
11 contacted employed people at all the different levels used in the
12 city service.
13 The conclusions I draw from analyzing this information is
14 as follows: The city's entry-level salary is about average for
15 the region; middle-level salaries are generally higher in the
16 city government plan than in private industry; but salaries at the
17 highest levels in private industry are better than city em-
18 ployees' pay.

1. Which of the following criticisms about the style in which this report is written is MOST valid?
   A. It is too informal.
   B. It is too concise.
   C. It is too choppy.
   D. The syntax is too complex.

1.____

2. Judging from the statements made in the report, the method followed by this employee in performing his research was
   A. *good*; he contacted a representative sample of businesses in the area
   B. *poor*; he should have drawn more definite conclusions
   C. *good*; he was persistent in collecting information
   D. *poor*; he did not make a thorough study

2.____

133

3. One sentence in this report contains a grammatical error. This sentence begins on line number
   A. 4   B. 7   C. 10   D. 14

4. The type of information given in this report which should be presented in footnotes or in an appendix is the
   A. purpose of the study
   B. specifics about the businesses contacted
   C. reference to the chart
   D. conclusions drawn by the author

5. The use of a graph to show statistical data in a report is SUPERIOR to a table because it
   A. features approximations
   B. emphasizes facts and relationships more dramatically
   C. presents data more accurately
   D. is easily understood by the average reader

6. Of the following, the degree of formality required of a written report in tone is MOST likely to depend on the
   A. subject matter of the report
   B. frequency of its occurrence
   C. amount of time available for its preparation
   D. audience for whom the report is intended

7. Of the following, a distinguishing characteristic of a written report intended for the head of your agency as compared to a report prepared for a lower-echelon staff member is that the report for the agency head should USUALLY include
   A. considerably more detail, especially statistical data
   B. the essential details in an abbreviated form
   C. all available source material
   D. an annotated bibliography

8. Assume that you are asked to write a lengthy report for use by the administrator of your agency, the subject of which is "The Impact of Proposed New Data Processing Operation on Line Personnel" in your agency. You decide that the *most* appropriate type of report for you to prepare is an analytical report, including recommendations.
   The MAIN reason for your decision is that
   A. the subject of the report is extremely complex
   B. large sums of money are involved
   C. the report is being prepared for the administrator
   D. you intend to include charts and graphs

9. Assume that you are preparing a report based on a survey dealing with the attitudes of employees in Division X regarding proposed new changes in compensating employees for working overtime. Three percent of the respondents to the survey voluntarily offer an unfavorable opinion on the method of assigning overtime work, a question not specifically asked of the employees.
On the basis of this information, the MOST appropriate and significant of the following comments for you to make in the report with regard to employees' attitudes on assigning overtime work is that
   A. an insignificant percentage of employees dislike the method of assigning overtime work
   B. three percent of the employees in Division X dislike the method of assigning overtime work
   C. three percent of the sample selected for the survey voiced an unfavorable opinion on the method of assigning overtime work
   D. some employees voluntarily voiced negative feelings about the method of assigning overtime work, making it impossible to determine the extent of this attitude

9._____

10. A supervisor should be able to prepare a report that is well-written and unambiguous.
Of the following sentences that might appear in a report, select the one which communicates MOST clearly the intent of its author.
   A. When your subordinates speak to a group of people, they should be well-informed.
   B. When he asked him to leave, SanMan King told him that he would refuse the request.
   C. Because he is a good worker, Foreman Jefferson assigned Assistant Foreman D'Agostino to replace him.
   D. Each of us is responsible for the actions of our subordinates.

10._____

11. In some reports, especially longer ones, a list of the resources (books, papers, magazines, etc.) used to prepare it is included. This list is called the
   A. accreditation   B. bibliography
   C. summary   D. glossary

11._____

12. Reports are usually divided into several sections, some of which are more necessary than others.
Of the following, the section which is ABSOLUTELY necessary to include in a report is
   A. a table of contents   B. the body
   C. an index   D. a bibliography

12._____

13. Suppose you are writing a report on an interview you have just completed with a particularly hostile applicant.
    Which of the following BEST describes what you should include in this report?
    A. What you think caused the applicant's hostile attitude during the interview
    B. Specific examples of the applicant's hostile remarks and behavior
    C. The relevant information uncovered during the interview
    D. A recommendation that the applicant's request be denied because of his hostility

14. When including recommendations in a report to your supervisor, which of the following is MOST important for you to do?
    A. Provide several alternative courses of action for each recommendation
    B. First present the supporting evidence, then the recommendations
    C. First present the recommendations, then the supporting evidence
    D. Make sure the recommendations arise logically out of the information in the report

15. It is often necessary that the writer of a report present facts and sufficient arguments to gain acceptance of the points, conclusions, or recommendations set forth in the report.
    Of the following, the LEAST advisable step to take in organizing a report, when such argumentation is the important factor, is a(n)
    A. elaborate expression of personal belief
    B. businesslike discussion of the problem as a whole
    C. orderly arrangement of convincing data
    D. reasonable explanation of the primary issues

16. In some types of reports, visual aids add interest, meaning, and support. They also provide an essential means of effectively communicating the message of the report.
    Of the following, the selection of the suitable visual aids to use with a report is LEAST dependent on the
    A. nature and scope of the report
    B. way in which the aid is to be used
    C. aid used in other reports
    D. prospective readers of the report

17. Visual aids used in a report may be placed either in the text material or in the appendix.
    Deciding where to put a chart, table, or any such aid should depend on the
    A. title of the report   B. purpose of the visual aid
    C. title of the visual aid   D. length of the report

18. A report is often revised several times before final preparation and distribution in an effort to make certain the report meets the needs of the situation for which it is designed.
    Which of the following is the BEST way for the author to be sure that a report covers the areas he intended?

A. Obtain a coworker's opinion
B. Compare it with a content checklist
C. Test it on a subordinate
D. Check his bibliography

19. In which of the following situations is an oral report preferable to a written report? When a(n)
    A. recommendation is being made for a future plan of action
    B. department head requests immediate information
    C. long-standing policy change is made
    D. analysis of complicated statistical data is involved

20. When an applicant is approved, the supervisor must fill in standard forms with certain information.
    The GREATEST advantage of using standard forms in this situation rather than having the supervisor write the report as he sees fit is that
    A. the report can be acted on quickly
    B. the report can be written without directions from a supervisor
    C. needed information is less likely to be left out of the report
    D. information that is written up this way is more likely to be verified

21. Assume that it is part of your job to prepare a monthly report for your unit head that eventually goes to the director. The report contains information on the number of applicants you have interviewed that have been approved and the number of applicants you have interviewed that have been turned down.
    Errors on such reports are serious because
    A. you are expected to be able to prove how many applicants you have interviewed each month
    B. accurate statistics are needed for effective management of the department
    C. they may not be discovered before the report is transmitted to the director
    D. they may result in loss to the applicants left out of the report

22. The frequency with which job reports are submitted should depend MAINLY on
    A. how comprehensive the report has to be
    B. the amount of information in the report
    C. the availability of an experienced man to write the report
    D. the importance of changes in the information included in the report

23. The CHIEF purpose in preparing an outline for a report is usually to insure that
    A. the report will be grammatically correct
    B. every point will be given equal emphasis
    C. principal and secondary points will be properly integrated
    D. the language of the report will be of the same level and include the same technical terms

24. The MAIN reason for requiring written job reports is to
    A. avoid the necessity of oral orders
    B. develop better methods of doing the work
    C. provide a permanent record of what was done
    D. increase the amount of work that can be done

24.____

25. Assume you are recommending in a report to your supervisor that a radical change in a standard maintenance procedure should be adopted.
    Of the following, the MOST important information to be included in this report is
    A. a list of the reasons for making this change
    B. the names of others who favor the change
    C. a complete description of the present procedure
    D. amount of training time needed for the new procedure

25.____

KEY (CORRECT ANSWERS)

1.	A		11.	B
2.	D		12.	B
3.	D		13.	C
4.	B		14.	D
5.	B		15.	A
6.	D		16.	C
7.	B		17.	B
8.	A		18.	B
9.	D		19.	B
10.	D		20.	C

21.	B
22.	D
23.	C
24.	C
25.	A

TEST 2

DIRECTIONS: Each question or incomplete statement is followed by several suggested answers or completions. Select the one that BEST answers the question or completes the statement. *PRINT THE LETTER OF THE CORRECT ANSWER IN THE SPACE AT THE RIGHT.*

1. It is often necessary that the writer of a report present facts and sufficient arguments to gain acceptance of the points, conclusions, or recommendations set forth in the report.
   Of the following, the LEAST advisable step to take in organizing a report, when such argumentation is the important factor, is a(n)
   A. elaborate expression of personal belief
   B. businesslike discussion of the problem as a whole
   C. orderly arrangement of convincing data
   D. reasonable explanation of the primary issues

   1.____

2. Of the following, the factor which is generally considered to be LEAST characteristic of a good control report is that it
   A. stresses performance that adheres to standard rather than emphasizing the exception
   B. supplies information intended to serve as the basis for corrective action
   C. provides feedback for the planning process
   D. includes data that reflect trends as well as current status

   2.____

3. An administrative assistant has been asked by his superior to write a concise, factual report with objective conclusions and recommendations based on facts assembled by other researchers.
   Of the following factors, the administrative assistant should give LEAST consideration to
   A. the educational level of the person or persons for whom the report is being prepared
   B. the use to be made of the report
   C. the complexity of the problem
   D. his own feelings about the importance of the problem

   3.____

4. When making a written report, it is often recommended that the findings or conclusions be presented near the beginning of the report.
   Of the following, the MOST important reason for doing this is that it
   A. facilitates organizing the material clearly
   B. assures that all the topics will be covered
   C. avoids unnecessary repetition of ideas
   D. prepares the reader for the facts that will follow

   4.____

5. You have been asked to write a report on methods of hiring and training new employees. Your report is going to be about ten pages long.
For the convenience of your readers, a brief summary of your findings should
   A. appear at the beginning of your report
   B. be appended to the report as a postscript
   C. be circulated in a separate memo
   D. be inserted in tabular form in the middle of your report

6. In preparing a report, the MAIN reason for writing an outline is usually to
   A. help organize thoughts in a logical sequence
   B. provide a guide for the typing of the report
   C. allow the ultimate user to review the report in advance
   D. ensure that the report is being prepared on schedule

7. The one of the following which is MOST appropriate as a reason for including footnotes in a report is to
   A. correct capitalization
   B. delete passages
   C. improve punctuation
   D. cite references

8. A completed formal report may contain all of the following EXCEPT
   A. a synopsis
   B. a preface
   C. marginal notes
   D. bibliographical references

9. Of the following, the MAIN use of proofreaders' marks is to
   A. explain corrections to be made
   B. indicate that a manuscript has been read and approved
   C. let the reader know who proofread the report
   D. indicate the format of the report

10. Informative, readable, and concise reports have been found to observe the following rules:
    Rule I. Keep the report short and easy to understand
    Rule II. Vary the length of sentences.
    Rule III. Vary the style of sentences so that, for example, they are not all just subject-verb, subject-verb.
    Consider this hospital laboratory report: The experiment was started in January. The apparatus was put together in six weeks. At that time, the synthesizing process was begun. The synthetic chemicals were separated. Then they were used in tests on patients.
    Which one of the following choices MOST accurately classifies the above rules into those which are violated by this report ad those which are not?
    A. II is violated, but I and III are not.
    B. III is violated, but I and II are not.
    C. II and III are violated, but I is not.
    D. I, II, and III are violated,

Questions 11-13.

DIRECTIONS: Questions 11 through 13 are based on the following example of a report. The report consists of eight numbered sentences, some of which are not consistent with the principles of good report writing.

(1) I interviewed Mrs. Loretta Crawford in Room 424 of County Hospital. (2) She had collapsed on the street and been brought into emergency. (3) She is an attractive woman with many friends judging by the cards she had received. (4) She did not know what her husband's last job had been, or what their present income was. (5) The first thing that Mrs. Crawford said was that she had never worked and that her husband was presently unemployed. (6) She did not know if they had any medical coverage or if they could pay the bill. (7) She said that her husband could not be reached by telephone but that he would be in to see her that afternoon. (8) I left word at the nursing station to be called when he arrived.

11. A good report should be arranged in logical order.
    Which of the following sentences from the report does NOT appear in its proper sequence in the report?
    A. 1   B. 4   C. 7   D. 8

12. Only material that is relevant to the main thought of a report should be included. Which of the following sentences from the report contains material which is LEAST relevant to this report? Sentence
    A. 3   B. 4   C. 6   D. 8

13. Reports should include all essential information.
    Of the following, the MOST important fact that is missing from this report is:
    A. Who was involved in the interview
    B. What was discovered at the interview
    C. When the interview took place
    D. Where the interview took place

Questions 14-15.

DIRECTIONS: Each of Questions 14 and 15 consists of four numbered sentences which constitute a paragraph in a report. They are not in the right order. Choose the numbered arrangement appearing after letter A, B, C, or D which is MOST logical and which BEST expresses the thought of the paragraph.

14. I. Congress made the commitment explicit in the Housing Act of 1949, establishing as a national goal the realization of a decent home and suitable environment for every American family.
    II. The result has been that the goal of decent home and suitable environment is still as far distant as ever for the disadvantaged urban family
    III. In spite of this action by Congress, federal housing programs have continued to be fragmented and grossly under-funded.
    IV. The passage of the National Housing Act signaled a new federal commitment to provide housing for the nation's citizens.

The CORRECT answer is:
A. I, IV, III, II   B. IV, I, III, II   C. IV, I, III, II   D. II, IV, I, III

15. I. The greater expense does not necessarily involve "exploitation," but it is often perceived as exploitative and unfair by those who are aware of the price differences involved, but unaware of operating costs.
    II. Ghetto residents believe they are "exploited" by local merchants, and evidence substantiates some of these beliefs.
    III. However, stores in low-income areas were more likely to be small independents, which could not achieve the economies available to supermarket chains and were, therefore, more likely to charge higher prices, and the customers were more likely to buy smaller-sized packages which are more expensive per unit of measure.
    IV. A study conducted in one city showed that distinctly higher prices were charged for goods sold in ghetto stores than in other areas.

    The CORRECT answer is:
    A. IV, II, I, III   B. IV, I, III, II   C. II, IV, III, I   D. II, III, IV, I

15.____

16. In organizing data to be presented in a formal report, the FIRST of the following steps should be
    A. determining the conclusions to be drawn
    B. establishing the time sequence of the data
    C. sorting and arranging like data into groups
    D. evaluating how consistently the data support the recommendations

16.____

17. All reports should be prepared with at least one copy so that
    A. there is one copy for your file
    B. there is a copy for your supervisor
    C. the report can be sent to more than one person
    D. the person getting the report can forward a copy to someone else

17.____

18. Before turning in a report of an investigation he has made, a supervisor discovers some additional information he did not include in this report. Whether he rewrites this report to include this additional information should PRIMARILY depend on the
    A. importance of the report itself
    B. number of people who will eventually review this report
    C. established policy covering the subject matter of the report
    D. bearing this new information has on the conclusions of the report

18.____

KEY (CORRECT ANSWERS)

1.	A	11.	B
2.	A	12.	A
3.	D	13.	C
4.	D	14.	B
5.	A	15.	C
6.	A	16.	C
7.	D	17.	A
8.	C	18.	D
9.	A		
10.	C		

PREPARING WRITTEN MATERIAL
EXAMINATION SECTION
TEST 1

DIRECTIONS: Each of the sentences in this test may be classified under one of the following four categories:
- A. Faulty because of incorrect grammar or word usage
- B. Faulty because of incorrect punctuation
- C. Faulty because of incorrect capitalization or incorrect spelling
- D. Correct

Examine each sentence carefully to determine under which of the above four options it is best classified. Then, in the space to the right, print the capital letter preceding the option which is the BEST of the four suggested above. (Note that each faulty sentence contains but one type of error. Consider a sentence to be correct if it contains none of the types of errors mentioned, even though there may be other correct ways of expressing the same thought.)

1. He sent the notice to the clerk who you hired yesterday.   1.____

2. It must be admitted, however that you were not informed of this change.   2.____

3. Only the employee who have served in this grade for at least two years are eligible for promotion.   3.____

4. The work was divided equally between she and Mary.   4.____

5. He thought that you were not available at that time.   5.____

6. When the messenger returns; please give him this package.   6.____

7. The new secretary prepared, typed, addressed, and delivered, the notices.   7.____

8. Walking into the room, his desk can be seen at the rear.   8.____

9. Although John has worked here longer than She, he produces a smaller amount of work.   9.____

10. She said she could of typed this report yesterday.   10.____

11. Neither one of these procedures are adequate for the efficient performance of this task.   11.____

12. The typewriter is the tool of the typist; the cash register, the tool of the cashier.   12.____

13. "The assignment must be completed as soon as possible" said the supervisor. 13._____

14. As you know, office handbooks are issued to all new Employees. 14._____

15. Writing a speech is sometimes easier than to deliver it before an audience. 15._____

16. Mr. Brown our accountant, will audit the accounts next week. 16._____

17. Give the assignment to whomever is able to do it most efficiently. 17._____

18. The supervisor expected either your or I to file these reports. 18._____

KEY (CORRECT ANSWERS)

1.	A	11.	A
2.	B	12.	C
3.	D	13.	B
4.	A	14.	C
5.	D	15.	A
6.	B	16.	B
7.	B	17.	A
8.	A	18.	A
9.	C		
10.	A		

TEST 2

DIRECTIONS: Each of the sentences in this test may be classified under one of the following four categories:
- A. Faulty because of incorrect grammar or word usage
- B. Faulty because of incorrect punctuation
- C. Faulty because of incorrect capitalization or incorrect spelling
- D. Correct

Examine each sentence carefully to determine under which of the above four options it is best classified. Then, in the space to the right, print the capital letter preceding the option which is the BEST of the four suggested above. (Note that each faulty sentence contains but one type of error. Consider a sentence to be correct if it contains none of the types of errors mentioned, even though there may be other correct ways of expressing the same thought.)

1. The fire apparently started in the storeroom, which is usually locked.   1._____
2. On approaching the victim, two bruises were noticed by this officer.   2._____
3. The officer, who was there examined the report with great care.   3._____
4. Each employee in the office had a seperate desk.   4._____
5. All employees including members of the clerical staff, were invited to the lecture.   5._____
6. The suggested Procedure is similar to the one now in use.   6._____
7. No one was more pleased with the new procedure than the chauffeur.   7._____
8. He tried to persaude her to change the procedure.   8._____
9. The total of the expenses charged to petty cash were high.   9._____
10. An understanding between him and I was finally reached.   10._____

KEY (CORRECT ANSWERS)

1. D   6. C
2. A   7. D
3. B   8. C
4. C   9. A
5. B   10. A

TEST 3

DIRECTIONS: Each of the sentences in this test may be classified under one of the following four categories:
  A. Faulty because of incorrect grammar or word usage
  B. Faulty because of incorrect punctuation
  C. Faulty because of incorrect capitalization or incorrect spelling
  D. Correct

Examine each sentence carefully to determine under which of the above four options it is best classified. Then, in the space to the right, print the capital letter preceding the option which is the BEST of the four suggested above. (Note that each faulty sentence contains but one type of error. Consider a sentence to be correct if it contains none of the types of errors mentioned, even though there may be other correct ways of expressing the same thought.)

1. They told both he and I that the prisoner had escaped. 1.____

2. Any superior officer, who, disregards the just complaint of his subordinates, is remiss in the performance of his duty. 2.____

3. Only those members of the national organization who resided in the Middle West attended the conference in Chicago. 3.____

4. We told him to give the national organization assignment to whoever was available. 4.____

5. Please do not disappoint and embarass us by not appearing in court. 5.____

6. Although the office's speech proved to be entertaining, the topic was not relevent to the main theme of the conference. 6.____

7. In February all new officers attended a training course in which they were learned in their principal duties and the fundamental operating procedure of the department. 7.____

8. I personally seen inmate Jones threaten inmates Smith and Green with bodily harm if they refused to participate in the plot. 8.____

9. To the layman, who on a chance visit to the prison observes everything functioning smoothly, the maintenance of prison discipline may seem to be a relatively easily realizable objective. 9.____

10. The prisoners in cell block fourty were forbidden to sit on the cell cots during the recreation hour. 10.____

KEY (CORRECT ANSWERS)

1. A
2. B
3. C
4. D
5. C
6. C
7. A
8. A
9. D
10. C

TEST 4

DIRECTIONS: Each of the sentences in this test may be classified under one of the following four categories:
    A. Faulty because of incorrect grammar or word usage
    B. Faulty because of incorrect punctuation
    C. Faulty because of incorrect capitalization or incorrect spelling
    D. Correct

Examine each sentence carefully to determine under which of the above four options it is best classified. Then, in the space to the right, print the capital letter preceding the option which is the BEST of the four suggested above. (Note that each faulty sentence contains but one type of error. Consider a sentence to be correct if it contains none of the types of errors mentioned, even though there may be other correct ways of expressing the same thought.)

1. I cannot encourage you any.   1.____
2. You always look well in those sort of clothes.   2.____
3. Shall we go to the park?   3.____
4. The man whome he introduced was Mr. Carey.   4.____
5. She saw the letter laying here this morning.   5.____
6. It should rain before the Afternoon is over.   6.____
7. They have already went home.   7.____
8. That Jackson will be elected is evident.   8.____
9. He does not hardly approve of us.   9.____
10. It was he, who won the prize.   10.____

KEY (CORRECT ANSWERS)

1. A   6. C
2. A   7. A
3. D   8. D
4. C   9. A
5. A   10. B

TEST 5

DIRECTIONS: Each of the sentences in this test may be classified under one of the following four categories:
- A. Faulty because of incorrect grammar or word usage
- B. Faulty because of incorrect punctuation
- C. Faulty because of incorrect capitalization or incorrect spelling
- D. Correct

Examine each sentence carefully to determine under which of the above four options it is best classified. Then, in the space to the right, print the capital letter preceding the option which is the BEST of the four suggested above. (Note that each faulty sentence contains but one type of error. Consider a sentence to be correct if it contains none of the types of errors mentioned, even though there may be other correct ways of expressing the same thought.)

1. Shall we go to the park.   1.____
2. They are, alike, in this particular way.   2.____
3. They gave the poor man sume food when he knocked on the door.   3.____
4. I regret the loss caused by the error.   4.____
5. The students' will have a new teacher.   5.____
6. They sweared to bring out all the facts.   6.____
7. He decided to open a branch store on 33rd street.   7.____
8. His speed is equal and more than that of a racehorse.   8.____
9. He felt very warm on that Summer day.   9.____
10. He was assisted by his friend, who lives in the next house.   10.____

KEY (CORRECT ANSWERS)

1.	B	6.	A
2.	B	7.	C
3.	C	8.	A
4.	D	9.	C
5.	B	10.	D

TEST 6

DIRECTIONS: Each of the sentences in this test may be classified under one of the following four categories:
- A. Faulty because of incorrect grammar or word usage
- B. Faulty because of incorrect punctuation
- C. Faulty because of incorrect capitalization or incorrect spelling
- D. Correct

Examine each sentence carefully to determine under which of the above four options it is best classified. Then, in the space to the right, print the capital letter preceding the option which is the BEST of the four suggested above. (Note that each faulty sentence contains but one type of error. Consider a sentence to be correct if it contains none of the types of errors mentioned, even though there may be other correct ways of expressing the same thought.)

1. The climate of New York is colder than California. 1.____
2. I shall wait for you on the corner. 2.____
3. Did we see the boy who, we think, is the leader. 3.____
4. Being a modest person, John seldom talks about his invention. 4.____
5. The gang is called the smith street bos. 5.____
6. He seen the man break into the store. 6.____
7. We expected to lay still there for quite a while. 7.____
8. He is considered to be the Leader of his organization. 8.____
9. Although I recieved an invitation, I won't go. 9.____
10. The letter must be here some place. 10.____

KEY (CORRECT ANSWERS)

1.	A	6.	A
2.	D	7.	A
3.	B	8.	C
4.	D	9.	C
5.	C	10.	A

TEST 7

DIRECTIONS: Each of the sentences in this test may be classified under one of the following four categories:
- A. Faulty because of incorrect grammar or word usage
- B. Faulty because of incorrect punctuation
- C. Faulty because of incorrect capitalization or incorrect spelling
- D. Correct

Examine each sentence carefully to determine under which of the above four options it is best classified. Then, in the space to the right, print the capital letter preceding the option which is the BEST of the four suggested above. (Note that each faulty sentence contains but one type of error. Consider a sentence to be correct if it contains none of the types of errors mentioned, even though there may be other correct ways of expressing the same thought.)

1. I though it to be he. 1._____
2. We expect to remain here for a long time. 2._____
3. The committee was agreed. 3._____
4. Two-thirds of the building are finished. 4._____
5. The water was froze. 5._____
6. Everyone of the salesmen must supply their own car. 6._____
7. Who is the author of Gone With the Wind? 7._____
8. He marched on and declaring that he would never surrender. 8._____
9. Who shall I say called? 9._____
10. Everyone has left but they. 10._____

KEY (CORRECT ANSWERS)

1.	A	6.	A
2.	D	7.	B
3.	D	8.	A
4.	A	9.	D
5.	A	10.	D

TEST 8

DIRECTIONS: Each of the sentences in this test may be classified under one of the following four categories:
    A. Faulty because of incorrect grammar or word usage
    B. Faulty because of incorrect punctuation
    C. Faulty because of incorrect capitalization or incorrect spelling
    D. Correct

Examine each sentence carefully to determine under which of the above four options it is best classified. Then, in the space to the right, print the capital letter preceding the option which is the BEST of the four suggested above. (Note that each faulty sentence contains but one type of error. Consider a sentence to be correct if it contains none of the types of errors mentioned, even though there may be other correct ways of expressing the same thought.)

1. Who did we give the order to?
2. Send your order in immediately.
3. I believe I paid the Bill.
4. I have not met but one person.
5. Why aren't Tom, and Fred, going to the dance?
6. What reason is there for him not going?
7. The seige of Malta was a tremendous event.
8. I was there yesterday I assure you
9. Your ukulele is better than mine.
10. No one was there only Mary.

KEY (CORRECT ANSWERS)

1.	A	6.	A
2.	D	7.	C
3.	C	8.	B
4.	A	9.	C
5.	B	10.	A

TEST 9

DIRECTIONS: In each of the following groups of sentences, one of the four sentences is faulty in grammar, punctuation, or capitalization. Select the INCORRECT sentence in each case.

1. A. If you had stood at home and done your homework, you would not have failed in arithmetic.
    B. Her affected manner annoyed every member of the audience.
    C. How will the new law affect our income taxes?
    D. The plants were not affected by the long, cold winter, but they succumbed to the drought of summer.

2. A. He is one of the most able men who have been in the Senate.
    B. It is he who is to blame for the lamentable mistake.
    C. Haven't you a helpful suggestion to make at this time?
    D. The money was robbed from the blind man's cup.

3. A. The amount of children in this school is steadily increasing.
    B. After taking an apple from the table, she went out to play.
    C. He borrowed a dollar from me.
    D. I had hoped my brother would arrive before me.

4. A. Whom do you think I hear from every week?
    B. Who do you think is the right man for the job?
    C. Who do you think I found in the room?
    D. He is the man whom we considered a good candidate for the presidency.

5. A. Quietly the puppy laid down before the fireplace.
    B. You have made your bed; now lie in it.
    C. I was badly sunburned because I had lain too long in the sun.
    D. I laid the doll on the bed and left the room.

KEY (CORRECT ANSWERS)

1. A
2. D
3. A
4. C
5. A

PREPARING WRITTEN MATERIAL
EXAMINATION SECTION
TEST 1

DIRECTIONS: Each of the sentences in this test may be classified under one of the following four categories:
- A. *Incorrect* because of faulty grammar or sentence structure
- B. *Incorrect* because of faulty punctuation
- C. *Incorrect* because of faulty capitalization
- D. *Correct*

Examine each sentence carefully to determine under which of the above four options it is best classified. Then, in the space at the right, print the capital letter preceding the option which is the BEST of the four suggested above.

(Each incorrect sentence contains but one type of error. Consider a sentence to be correct if it contains none of the types of errors mentioned, even though there may be other correct ways of expressing the same thought.)

1. This fact, together with those brought out at the previous meeting, prove that the schedule is satisfactory to the employees. 1.____

2. Like many employees in scientific fields, the work of bookkeepers and accountants requires accuracy and neatness. 2.____

3. "What can I do for you," the secretary asked as she motioned to the visitor to take a seat. 3.____

4. Our representative, Mr. Charles will call on you next week to determine whether or not your claim has merit. 4.____

5. We expect you to return in the spring; please do not disappoint us. 5.____

6. Any supervisor, who disregards the just complaints of his subordinates, is remiss in the performance of his duty. 6.____

7. Because she took less than an hour for lunch is no reason for permitting her to leave before five o'clock. 7.____

8. "Miss Smith," said the supervisor, "Please arrange a meeting of the staff for two o'clock on Monday." 8.____

9. A private company's vacation and sick leave allowance usually differs considerably from a public agency. 9.____

10. Therefore, in order to increase the efficiency of operations in the department, a report on the recommended changes in procedures was presented to the departmental committee in charge of the program. 10.____

11. We told him to assign the work to whoever was available. 11._____

12. Since John was the most efficient of any other employee in the bureau, he received the highest service rating. 12._____

13. Only those members of the national organization who resided in the middle West attended the conference in Chicago. 13._____

14. The question of whether the office manager has as yet attained, or indeed can ever hope to secure professional status is one which has been discussed for years. 14._____

15. No one knew who to blame for the error which, we later discovered, resulted in a considerable loss of time. 15._____

KEY (CORRECT ANSWERS)

1.	A	6.	B	11.	D
2.	A	7.	A	12.	A
3.	B	8.	C	13.	C
4.	B	9.	A	14.	B
5.	D	10.	D	15.	A

TEST 2

DIRECTIONS: Each of the sentences in this test may be classified under one of the following four categories:
- A. *Incorrect* because of faulty grammar or sentence structure
- B. *Incorrect* because of faulty punctuation
- C. *Incorrect* because of faulty capitalization
- D. *Correct*

1. The National alliance of Businessmen is trying to persuade private businesses to hire youth in the summertime.   1.____

2. The supervisor who is on vacation, is in charge of processing vouchers.   2.____

3. The activity of the committee at its conferences is always stimulating.   3.____

4. After checking the addresses again, the letters went to the mailroom.   4.____

5. The director, as well as the employees, are interested in sharing the dividends.   5.____

KEY (CORRECT ANSWERS)

1. C
2. B
3. D
4. A
5. A

TEST 3

DIRECTIONS: In each of the following groups of sentences, one of the four sentences is faulty in grammar, punctuation, or capitalization. Select the INCORRECT sentence in each case.

1.
   A. Sailing down the bay was a thrilling experience for me.
   B. He was not consulted about your joining the club.
   C. This story is different than the one I told you yesterday.
   D. There is no doubt about his being the best player.

   1.____

2.
   A. He maintains there is but one road to world peace.
   B. It is common knowledge that a child sees much he is not supposed to see.
   C. Much of the bitterness might have been avoided if arbitration had been resorted to earlier in the meeting.
   D. The man decided it would be advisable to marry a girl somewhat younger than him.

   2.____

3.
   A. In this book, the incident I liked least is where the hero tries to put out the forest fire.
   B. Learning a foreign language will undoubtedly give a person a better understanding of his mother tongue.
   C. His actions made us wonder what he planned to do next.
   D. Because of the war, we were unable to travel during the summer vacation.

   3.____

4.
   A. The class had no sooner become interested in the lesson than the dismissal bell rang.
   B. There is little agreement about the kind of world to be planned at the peace conference.
   C. "Today," said the teacher, "we shall read 'The Wind in the Willows,' I am sure you'll like it.
   D. The terms of the legal settlement of the family quarrel handicapped both sides for many years.

   4.____

5.
   A. I was so surprised that I was not able to say a word.
   B. She is taller than any other member of the class.
   C. It would be much more preferable if you were never seen in his company.
   D. We had no choice but to excuse her for being late.

   5.____

KEY (CORRECT ANSWERS)

1. C
2. D
3. A
4. C
5. C

TEST 4

DIRECTIONS: In each of the following groups of sentences, one of the four sentences is faulty in grammar, punctuation, or capitalization. Select the INCORRECT sentence in each case.

1. A. Please send me these data at the earliest opportunity.
   B. The loss of their material proved to be a severe handicap.
   C. My principal objection to this plan is that it is impracticable.
   D. The doll had laid in the rain for an hour and was ruined.

   1.____

2. A. The garden scissors, left out all night in the rain, were in a badly rusted condition.
   B. The girls felt bad about the misunderstanding which had arisen
   C. Sitting near the campfire, the old man told John and I about many exciting adventures he had had.
   D. Neither of us is in a position to undertake a task of that magnitude.

   2.____

3. A. The general concluded that one of the three roads would lead to the besieged city.
   B. The children didn't, as a rule, do hardly anything beyond what they were told to do.
   C. The reason the girl gave for her negligence was that she had acted on the spur of the moment.
   D. The daffodils and tulips look beautiful in that blue vase.

   3.____

4. A. If I was ten years older, I should be interested in this work.
   B. Give the prize to whoever has drawn the best picture.
   C. When you have finished reading the book, take it back to the library.
   D. My drawing is as good as or better than yours.

   4.____

5. A. He asked me whether the substance was animal or vegetable.
   B. An apple which is unripe should not be eaten by a child.
   C. That was an insult to me who am your friend.
   D. Some spy must of reported the matter to the enemy.

   5.____

6. A. Limited time makes quoting the entire message impossible.
   B. Who did she say was going?
   C. The girls in your class have dressed more dolls this year than we.
   D. There was such a large amount of books on the floor that I couldn't find a place for my rocking chair.

   6.____

7. A. What with his sleeplessness and his ill health, he was unable to assume any responsibility for the success of the meeting.
   B. If I had been born in February, I should be celebrating my birthday soon.
   C. In order to prevent breakage, she placed a sheet of paper between each of the plates when she packed them.
   D. After the spring shower, the violets smelled very sweet.

   7.____

8. A. He had laid the book down very reluctantly before the end of the lesson.
    B. The dog, I am sorry to say, had lain on the bed all night.
    C. The cloth was first lain on a flat surface; then it was pressed with a hot iron.
    D. While we were in Florida, we lay in the sun until we were noticeably tanned.

9. A. If John was in New York during the recent holiday season, I have no doubt he spent most of the time with his parents.
    B. How could he enjoy the television program; the dog was barking and the baby was crying.
    C. When the problem was explained to the class, he must have been asleep.
    D. She wished that her new dress were finished so that she could go to the party.

10. A. The engine not only furnishes power but light and heat as well.
    B. You're aware that we've forgotten whose guilt was established, aren't you?
    C. Everybody knows that the woman made many sacrifices for her children.
    D. A man with his dog and gun is a familiar sight in this neighborhood.

KEY (CORRECT ANSWERS)

1. D 6. D
2. C 7. B
3. B 8. C
4. A 9. B
5. D 10. A

TEST 5

DIRECTIONS: Each of Questions 1 through 5 consists of a sentence which may be classified appropriately under one of the following four categories:
- A. *Incorrect* because of faulty grammar
- B. *Incorrect* because of faulty punctuation
- C. *Incorrect* because of faulty spelling
- D. *Correct*

Examine each sentence carefully. Then, print in the space at the right the letter preceding the category which is the BEST of the four suggested above
(Note: Each incorrect sentence contains only one type of error. Consider a sentence correct if it contains no errors, although there may be other correct ways of writing the sentence.)

1. Of the two employees, the one in our office is the most efficient. 1.____

2. No one can apply or even understand, the new rules and regulations. 2.____

3. A large amount of supplies were stored in the empty office. 3.____

4. If an employee is occassionally asked to work overtime, he should do so willingly. 4.____

5. It is true that the new procedures are difficult to use but, we are certain that you will learn them quickly. 5.____

6. The office manager said that he did not know who would be given a large allotment under the new plan. 6.____

7. It was at the supervisor's request that the clerk agreed to postpone his vacation. 7.____

8. We do not believe that it is necessary for both he and the clerk to attend the conference. 8.____

9. All employees, who display perseverance, will be given adequate recognition. 9.____

10. He regrets that some of us employees are dissatisfied with our new assignments. 10.____

11. "Do you think that the raise was merited," asked the supervisor? 11.____

12. The new manual of procedure is a valuable supplament to our rules and regulations. 12.____

13. The typist admitted that she had attempted to pursuade the other employees to assist her in her work. 13.____

2 (#5)

14. The supervisor asked that all amendments to the regulations be handled by you and I.   14.____

15. The custodian seen the boy who broke the window.   15.____

KEY (CORRECT ANSWERS)

1.	A	6.	D	11.	B
2.	B	7.	D	12.	C
3.	A	8.	A	13.	C
4.	C	9.	B	14.	A
5.	B	10.	D	15.	A

PHILOSOPHY, PRINCIPLES, PRACTICES, AND TECHNICS OF SUPERVISION, ADMINISTRATION, MANAGEMENT, AND ORGANIZATION

TABLE OF CONTENTS

	Page
MEANING OF SUPERVISION	1
THE OLD AND THE NEW SUPERVISION	1
THE EIGHT (8) BASIC PRINCIPLES OF THE NEW SUPERVISION	1
I. Principle of Responsibility	1
II. Principle of Authority	2
III. Principle of Self-Growth	2
IV. Principle of Individual Worth	2
V. Principle of Creative Leadership	2
VI. Principle of Success and Failure	2
VII. Principle of Science	3
VIII. Principle of Cooperation	3
WHAT IS ADMINISTRATION?	3
I. Practices Commonly Classed as "Supervisory"	3
II. Practices Commonly Classed as "Administrative"	3
III. Practices Commonly Classed as Both "Supervisory" and "Administrative"	4
RESPONSIBILITIES OF THE SUPERVISOR	4
COMPETENCIES OF THE SUPERVISOR	4
THE PROFESSIONAL SUPERVISOR-EMPLOYEE RELATIONSHIP	4
MINI-TEXT IN SUPERVISION, ADMINISTRATION, MANAGEMENT, AND ORGANIZATION	5
I. Brief Highlights	5
A. Levels of Management	6
B. What the Supervisor Must Learn	6
C. A Definition of Supervision	6
D. Elements of the Team Concept	6
E. Principles of Organization	6
F. The Four Important Parts of Every Job	7
G. Principles of Delegation	7
H. Principles of Effective Communications	7
I. Principles of Work Improvement	7
J. Areas of Job Improvement	7
K. Seven Key Points in Making Improvements	8

	L.	Corrective Techniques for Job Improvement	8
	M.	A Planning Checklist	8
	N.	Five Characteristics of Good Directions	9
	O.	Types of Directions	9
	P.	Controls	9
	Q.	Orienting the New Employee	9
	R.	Checklist for Orienting New Employees	9
	S.	Principles of Learning	10
	T.	Causes of Poor Performance	10
	U.	Four Major Steps in On-the-Job Instructions	10
	V.	Employees Want Five Things	10
	W.	Some Don'ts in Regard to Praise	11
	X.	How to Gain Your Workers' Confidence	11
	Y.	Sources of Employee Problems	11
	Z.	The Supervisor's Key to Discipline	11
	AA.	Five Important Processes of Management	12
	BB.	When the Supervisor Fails to Plan	12
	CC.	Fourteen General Principles of Management	12
	DD.	Change	12
II.	Brief Topical Summaries		13
	A.	Who/What is the Supervisor?	13
	B.	The Sociology of Work	13
	C.	Principles and Practices of Supervision	14
	D.	Dynamic Leadership	14
	E.	Processes for Solving Problems	15
	F.	Training for Results	15
	G.	Health, Safety, and Accident Prevention	16
	H.	Equal Employment Opportunity	16
	I.	Improving Communications	16
	J.	Self-Development	17
	K.	Teaching and Training	17
		1. The Teaching Process	17
		a. Preparation	17
		b. Presentation	18
		c. Summary	18
		d. Application	18
		e. Evaluation	18
		2. Teaching Methods	18
		a. Lecture	18
		b. Discussion	18
		c. Demonstration	19
		d. Performance	19
		e. Which Method to Use	19

PHILOSOPHY, PRINCIPLES, PRACTICES, AND TECHNICS
OF
SUPERVISION, ADMINISTRATION, MANAGEMENT, AND ORGANIZATION

MEANING OF SUPERVISION

The extension of the democratic philosophy has been accompanied by an extension in the scope of supervision. Modern leaders and supervisors no longer think of supervision in the narrow sense of being confined chiefly to visiting employees, supplying materials, or rating the staff. They regard supervision as being intimately related to all the concerned agencies of society, they speak of the supervisor's function in terms of "growth," rather than the "improvement" of employees.

This modern concept of supervision may be defined as follows: Supervision is leadership and the development of leadership within groups which are cooperatively engaged in inspection, research, training, guidance, and evaluation.

THE OLD AND THE NEW SUPERVISION

TRADITIONAL
1. Inspection
2. Focused on the employee
3. Visitation
4. Random and haphazard
5. Imposed and authoritarian
6. One person usually

MODERN
1. Study and analysis
2. Focused on aims, materials, methods, supervisors, employees, environment
3. Demonstrations, intervisitation, workshops, directed reading, bulletins, etc.
4. Definitely organized and planned (scientific)
5. Cooperative and democratic
6. Many persons involved (creative)

THE EIGHT (8) BASIC PRINCIPLES OF THE NEW SUPERVISION

I. Principle of Responsibility
    Authority to act and responsibility for acting must be joined.
    A. If you give responsibility, give authority.
    B. Define employee duties clearly.
    C. Protect employees from criticism by others.
    D. Recognize the rights as well as obligations of employees.
    E. Achieve the aims of a democratic society insofar as it is possible within the area of your work.
    F. Establish a situation favorable to training and learning.
    G. Accept ultimate responsibility for everything done in your section, unit, office, division, department.
    H. Good administration and good supervision are inseparable.

II. Principle of Authority
The success of the supervisor is measured by the extent to which the power of authority is not used.
   A. Exercise simplicity and informality in supervision
   B. Use the simplest machinery of supervision
   C. If it is good for the organization as a whole, it is probably justified.
   D. Seldom be arbitrary or authoritative.
   E. Do not base your work on the power of position or of personality.
   F. Permit and encourage the free expression of opinions.

III. Principle of Self-Growth
The success of the supervisor is measured by the extent to which, and the speed with which, he is no longer needed.
   A. Base criticism on principles, not on specifics.
   B. Point out higher activities to employees.
   C. Train for self-thinking by employees to meet new situations.
   D. Stimulate initiative, self-reliance, and individual responsibility
   E. Concentrate on stimulating the growth of employees rather than on removing defects.

IV. Principle of Individual Worth
Respect for the individual is a paramount consideration in supervision.
   A. Be human and sympathetic in dealing with employees.
   B. Don't nag about things to be done.
   C. Recognize the individual differences among employees and seek opportunities to permit best expression of each personality.

V. Principle of Creative Leadership
The best supervision is that which is not apparent to the employee.
   A. Stimulate, don't drive employees to creative action.
   B. Emphasize doing good things.
   C. Encourage employees to do what they do best.
   D. Do not be too greatly concerned with details of subject or method.
   E. Do not be concerned exclusively with immediate problems and activities.
   F. Reveal higher activities and make them both desired and maximally possible.
   G. Determine procedures in the light of each situation but see that these are derived from a sound basic philosophy.
   H. Aid, inspire, and lead so as to liberate the creative spirit latent in all good employees.

VI. Principle of Success and Failure
There are no unsuccessful employees, only unsuccessful supervisors who have failed to give proper leadership.
   A. Adapt suggestions to the capacities, attitudes, and prejudices of employees.
   B. Be gradual, be progressive, be persistent.
   C. Help the employee find the general principle; have the employee apply his own problem to the general principle.
   D. Give adequate appreciation for good work and honest effort.
   E. Anticipate employee difficulties and help to prevent them.
   F. Encourage employees to do the desirable things they will do anyway.
   G. Judge your supervision by the results it secures.

VII. Principle of Science
Successful supervision is scientific, objective, and experimental. It is based on facts, not on prejudices.
   A. Be cumulative in results.
   B. Never divorce your suggestions from the goals of training.
   C. Don't be impatient of results.
   D. Keep all matters on a professional, not a personal, level.
   E. Do not be concerned exclusively with immediate problems and activities.
   F. Use objective means of determining achievement and rating where possible.

VIII. Principle of Cooperation
Supervision is a cooperative enterprise between supervisor and employee.
   A. Begin with conditions as they are.
   B. Ask opinions of all involved when formulating policies.
   C. Organization is as good as its weakest link.
   D. Let employees help to determine policies and department programs.
   E. Be approachable and accessible—physically and mentally.
   F. Develop pleasant social relationships.

WHAT IS ADMINISTRATION

Administration is concerned with providing the environment, the material facilities, and the operational procedures that will promote the maximum growth and development of supervisors and employees. (Organization is an aspect and a concomitant of administration.)

There is no sharp line of demarcation between supervision and administration; these functions are intimately interrelated and, often, overlapping. They are complementary activities.

I. Practices Commonly Classed as "Supervisory"
   A. Conducting employees' conferences
   B. Visiting sections, units, offices, divisions, departments
   C. Arranging for demonstrations
   D. Examining plans
   E. Suggesting professional reading
   F. Interpreting bulletins
   G. Recommending in-service training courses
   H. Encouraging experimentation
   I. Appraising employee morale
   J. Providing for intervisitation

II. Practices Commonly Classified as "Administrative"
   A. Management of the office
   B. Arrangement of schedules for extra duties
   C. Assignment of rooms or areas
   D. Distribution of supplies
   E. Keeping records and reports
   F. Care of audio-visual materials
   G. Keeping inventory records
   H. Checking record cards and books

I. Programming special activities
   J. Checking on the attendance and punctuality of employees

III. Practices Commonly Classified as Both "Supervisory" and "Administrative"
   A. Program construction
   B. Testing or evaluating outcomes
   C. Personnel accounting
   D. Ordering instructional materials

RESPONSIBILITIES OF THE SUPERVISOR

A person employed in a supervisory capacity must constantly be able to improve his own efficiency and ability. He represent the employer to the employees and only continuous self-examination can make him a capable supervisor.

Leadership and training are the supervisor's responsibility. An efficient working unit is one in which the employees work with the supervisor. It is his job to bring out the best in his employees. He must always be relaxed, courteous, and calm in his association with his employees. Their feelings are important, and a harsh attitude does not develop the most efficient employees.

COMPETENCES OF THE SUPERVISOR

   I. Complete knowledge of the duties and responsibilities of his position.
   II. To be able to organize a job, plan ahead, and carry through.
   III. To have self-confidence and initiative.
   IV. To be able to handle the unexpected situation and make quick decisions.
   V. To be able to properly train subordinates in the positions they are best suited for.
   VI. To be able to keep good human relations among his subordinates.
   VII. To be able to keep good human relations between his subordinates and himself and to earn their respect and trust.

THE PROFESSIONAL SUPERVISOR-EMPLOYEE RELATIONSHIP

There are two kinds of efficiency: one kind is only apparent and is produced in organizations through the exercise of mere discipline; this is but a simulation of the second, or true, efficiency which springs from spontaneous cooperation. If you are a manager, no matter how great or small your responsibility, it is your job, in the final analysis, to create and develop this involuntary cooperation among the people whom you supervise. For, no matter how powerful a combination of money, machines, and materials a company may have, this is a dead and sterile thing without a team of willing, thinking, and articulate people to guide it.

The following 21 points are presented as indicative of the exemplary basic relationship that should exist between supervisor and employee:

1. Each person wants to be liked and respected by his fellow employee and wants to be treated with consideration and respect by his superior.
2. The most competent employee will make an error. However, in a unit where good relations exist between the supervisor and his employees, tenseness and fear do not exist. Thus, errors are not hidden or covered up, and the efficiency of a unit is not impaired.

3. Subordinates resent rules, regulations, or orders that are unreasonable or unexplained.
4. Subordinates are quick to resent unfairness, harshness, injustices, and favoritism.
5. An employee will accept responsibility if he knows that he will be complimented for a job well done, and not too harshly chastised for failure; that his supervisor will check the cause of the failure, and, if it was the supervisor's fault, he will assume the blame therefore. If it was the employee's fault, his supervisor will explain the correct method or means of handling the responsibility.
6. An employee wants to receive credit for a suggestion he has made, that is used. If a suggestion cannot be used, the employee is entitled to an explanation. The supervisor should not say "no" and close the subject.
7. Fear and worry slow up a worker's ability. Poor working environment can impair his physical and mental health. A good supervisor avoids forceful methods, threats, and arguments to get a job done.
8. A forceful supervisor is able to train his employees individually and as a team, and is able to motivate them in the proper channels.
9. A mature supervisor is able to properly evaluate his subordinates and to keep them happy and satisfied.
10. A sensitive supervisor will never patronize his subordinates.
11. A worthy supervisor will respect his employees' confidences.
12. Definite and clear-cut responsibilities should be assigned to each executive.
13. Responsibility should always be coupled with corresponding authority.
14. No change should be made in the scope or responsibilities of a position without a definite understanding to that effect on the part of all persons concerned.
15. No executive or employee, occupying a single position in the organization, should be subject to definite orders from more than one source.
16. Orders should never be given to subordinates over the head of a responsible executive. Rather than do this, the officer in question should be supplanted.
17. Criticisms of subordinates should, whoever possible, be made privately, and in no case should a subordinate be criticized in the presence of executives or employees of equal or lower rank.
18. No dispute or difference between executives or employees as to authority or responsibilities should be considered too trivial for prompt and careful adjudication.
19. Promotions, wage changes, and disciplinary action should always be approved by the executive immediately superior to the one directly responsible.
20. No executive or employee should ever be required, or expected, to be at the same time an assistant to, and critic of, another.
21. Any executive whose work is subject to regular inspection should, wherever practicable, be given the assistance and facilities necessary to enable him to maintain an independent check of the quality of his work.

MINI-TEXT IN SUPERVISION, ADMINISTRATION, MANAGEMENT, AND ORGANIZATION

I. Brief Highlights

Listed concisely and sequentially are major headings and important data in the field for quick recall and review.

A. Levels of Management
Any organization of some size has several levels of management. In terms of a ladder, the levels are:

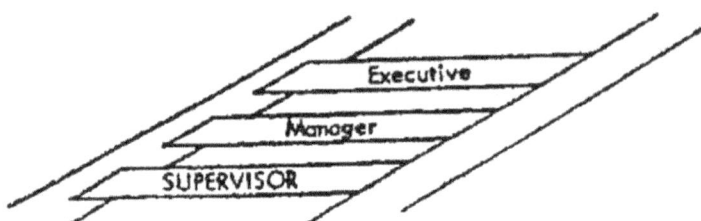

The first level is very important because it is the beginning point of management leadership.

B. What the Supervisor Must Learn
A supervisor must learn to:
1. Deal with people and their differences
2. Get the job done through people
3. Recognize the problems when they exist
4. Overcome obstacles to good performance
5. Evaluate the performance of people
6. Check his own performance in terms of accomplishment

C. A Definition of Supervisor
The term supervisor means any individual having authority, in the interests of the employer, to hire, transfer, suspend, lay-off, recall, promote, discharge, assign, reward, or discipline other employees or responsibility to direct them, or to adjust their grievances, or effectively to recommend such action, if, in connection with the foregoing, exercise of such authority is not of a merely routine or clerical nature but requires the use of independent judgment.

D. Elements of the Team Concept
What is involved in teamwork? The component parts are:
1. Members
2. A leader
3. Goals
4. Plans
5. Cooperation
6. Spirit

E. Principles of Organization
1. A team member must know what his job is.
2. Be sure that the nature and scope of a job are understood.
3. Authority and responsibility should be carefully spelled out.
4. A supervisor should be permitted to make the maximum number of decisions affecting his employees.
5. Employees should report to only one supervisor.
6. A supervisor should direct only as many employees as he can handle effectively.
7. An organization plan should be flexible.

8. Inspection and performance of work should be separate.
9. Organizational problems should receive immediate attention.
10. Assign work in line with ability and experience.

F. The Four Important Parts of Every Job
1. Inherent in every job is the *accountability* for results.
2. A second set of factors in every job is *responsibilities*.
3. Along with duties and responsibilities one must have the *authority* to act within certain limits without obtaining permission to proceed.
4. No job exists in a vacuum. The supervisor is surrounded by key *relationships*.

G. Principles of Delegation
Where work is delegated for the first time, the supervisor should think in terms of these questions:
1. Who is best qualified to do this?
2. Can an employee improve his abilities by doing this?
3. How long should an employee spend on this?
4. Are there any special problems for which he will need guidance?
5. How broad a delegation can I make?

H. Principles of Effective Communications
1. Determine the media.
2. To whom directed?
3. Identification and source authority.
4. Is communication understood?

I. Principles of Work Improvement
1. Most people usually do only the work which is assigned to them.
2. Workers are likely to fit assigned work into the time available to perform it.
3. A good workload usually stimulates output.
4. People usually do their best work when they know that results will be reviewed or inspected.
5. Employees usually feel that someone else is responsible for conditions of work, workplace layout, job methods, type of tools/equipment, and other such factors.
6. Employees are usually defensive about their job security.
7. Employees have natural resistance to change.
8. Employees can support or destroy a supervisor.
9. A supervisor usually earns the respect of his people through his personal example of diligence and efficiency.

J. Areas of Job Improvement
The areas of job improvement are quite numerous, but the most common ones which a supervisor can identify and utilize are:
1. Departmental layout
2. Flow of work
3. Workplace layout
4. Utilization of manpower
5. Work methods
6. Materials handling

7. Utilization
8. Motion economy

K. Seven Key Points in Making Improvements
1. Select the job to be improved
2. Study how it is being done now
3. Question the present method
4. Determine actions to be taken
5. Chart proposed method
6. Get approval and apply
7. Solicit worker participation

l. Corrective Techniques of Job Improvement
Specific Problems
1. Size of workload
2. Inability to meet schedules
3. Strain and fatigue
4. Improper use of men and skills
5. Waste, poor quality, unsafe conditions
6. Bottleneck conditions that hinder output
7. Poor utilization of equipment and machine
8. Efficiency and productivity of labor

General Improvement
1. Departmental layout
2. Flow of work
3. Work plan layout
4. Utilization of manpower
5. Work methods
6. Materials handling
7. Utilization of equipment
8. Motion economy

Corrective Techniques
1. Study with scale model
2. Flow chart study
3. Motion analysis
4. Comparison of units produced to standard allowance
5. Methods analysis
6. Flow chart and equipment study
7. Down time vs. running time
8. Motion analysis

M. A Planning Checklist
1. Objectives
2. Controls
3. Delegations
4. Communications
5. Resources
6. Manpower

7. Equipment
8. Supplies and materials
9. Utilization of time
10. Safety
11. Money
12. Work
13. Timing of improvements

N. Five Characteristics of Good Directions
In order to get results, directions must be:
1. Possible of accomplishment
2. Agreeable with worker interests
3. Related to mission
4. Planned and complete
5. Unmistakably clear

O. Types of Directions
1. Demands or direct orders
2. Requests
3. Suggestion or implication
4. volunteering

P. Controls
A typical listing of the overall areas in which the supervisor should establish controls might be:
1. Manpower
2. Materials
3. Quality of work
4. Quantity of work
5. Time
6. Space
7. Money
8. Methods

Q. Orienting the New Employee
1. Prepare for him
2. Welcome the new employee
3. Orientation for the job
4. Follow-up

R. Checklist for Orienting New Employees   Yes   No
1. Do you appreciate the feelings of new employees
   when they first report for work?   ___   ___
2. Are you aware of the fact that the new employee must
   make a big adjustment to his job?   ___   ___
3. Have you given him good reasons for liking the job and
   the organization?   ___   ___
4. Have you prepared for his first day on the job?   ___   ___
5. Did you welcome him cordially and make him feel needed?   ___   ___

	Yes	No
6. Did you establish rapport with him so that he feels free to talk and discuss matters with you?	___	___
7. Did you explain his job to him and his relationship to you?	___	___
8. Does he know that his work will be evaluated periodically on a basis that is fair and objective?	___	___
9. Did you introduce him to his fellow workers in such a way that they are likely to accept him?	___	___
10. Does he know what employee benefits he will receive?	___	___
11. Does he understand the importance of being on the job and what to do if he must leave his duty station?	___	___
12. Has he been impressed with the importance of accident prevention and safe practice?	___	___
13. Does he generally know his way around the department?	___	___
14. Is he under the guidance of a sponsor who will teach the right way of doing things?	___	___
15. Do you plan to follow-up so that he will continue to adjust successfully to his job?	___	___

S. Principles of Learning
   1. Motivation
   2. Demonstration or explanation
   3. Practice

T. Causes of Poor Performance
   1. Improper training for job
   2. Wrong tools
   3. Inadequate directions
   4. Lack of supervisory follow-up
   5. Poor communications
   6. Lack of standards of performance
   7. Wrong work habits
   8. Low morale
   9. Other

U. Four Major Steps in On-The-Job Instruction
   1. Prepare the worker
   2. Present the operation
   3. Tryout performance
   4. Follow-up

V. Employees Want Five Things
   1. Security
   2. Opportunity
   3. Recognition
   4. Inclusion
   5. Expression

W. Some Don'ts in Regard to Praise
1. Don't praise a person for something he hasn't done.
2. Don't praise a person unless you can be sincere.
3. Don't be sparing in praise just because your superior withholds it from you.
4. Don't let too much time elapse between good performance and recognition of it

X. How to Gain Your Workers' Confidence
Methods of developing confidence include such things as:
1. Knowing the interests, habits, hobbies of employees
2. Admitting your own inadequacies
3. Sharing and telling of confidence in others
4. Supporting people when they are in trouble
5. Delegating matters that can be well handled
6. Being frank and straightforward about problems and working conditions
7. Encouraging others to bring their problems to you
8. Taking action on problems which impede worker progress

Y. Sources of Employee Problems
On-the-job causes might be such things as:
1. A feeling that favoritism is exercised in assignments
2. Assignment of overtime
3. An undue amount of supervision
4. Changing methods or systems
5. Stealing of ideas or trade secrets
6. Lack of interest in job
7. Threat of reduction in force
8. Ignorance or lack of communications
9. Poor equipment
10. Lack of knowing how supervisor feels toward employee
11. Shift assignments

Off-the-job problems might have to do with:
1. Health
2. Finances
3. Housing
4. Family

Z. The Supervisor's Key to Discipline
There are several key points about discipline which the supervisor should keep in mind:
1. Job discipline is one of the disciplines of life and is directed by the supervisor.
2. It is more important to correct an employee fault than to fix blame for it.
3. Employee performance is affected by problems both on the job and off.
4. Sudden or abrupt changes in behavior can be indications of important employee problems.
5. Problems should be dealt with as soon as possible after they are identified.
6. The attitude of the supervisor may have more to do with solving problems than the techniques of problem solving.
7. Correction of employee behavior should be resorted to only after the supervisor is sure that training or counseling will not be helpful.

8. Be sure to document your disciplinary actions.
9. Make sure that you are disciplining on the basis of facts rather than personal feelings.
10. Take each disciplinary step in order, being careful not to make snap judgments, or decisions based on impatience.

AA. Five Important Processes of Management
1. Planning
2. Organizing
3. Scheduling
4. Controlling
5. Motivating

BB. When the Supervisor Fails to Plan
1. Supervisor creates impression of not knowing his job
2. May lead to excessive overtime
3. Job runs itself—supervisor lacks control
4. Deadlines and appointments missed
5. Parts of the work go undone
6. Work interrupted by emergencies
7. Sets a bad example
8. Uneven workload creates peaks and valleys
9. Too much time on minor details at expense of more important tasks

CC. Fourteen General Principles of Management
1. Division of work
2. Authority and responsibility
3. Discipline
4. Unity of command
5. Unity of direction
6. Subordination of individual interest to general interest
7. Remuneration of personnel
8. Centralization
9. Scalar chain
10. Order
11. Equity
12. Stability of tenure of personnel
13. Initiative
14. Esprit de corps

DD. Change

Bringing about change is perhaps attempted more often, and yet less well understood, than anything else the supervisor does. How do people generally react to change? (People tend to resist change that is imposed upon them by other individuals or circumstances.

Change is characteristic of every situation. It is a part of every real endeavor where the efforts of people are concerned.

1. Why do people resist change?
   People may resist change because of:
   a. Fear of the unknown
   b. Implied criticism
   c. Unpleasant experiences in the past
   d. Fear of loss of status
   e. Threat to the ego
   f. Fear of loss of economic stability

2. How can we best overcome the resistance to change?
   In initiating change, take these steps:
   a. Get ready to sell
   b. Identify sources of help
   c. Anticipate objections
   d. Sell benefits
   e. Listen in depth
   f. Follow up

II. Brief Topical Summaries

   A. Who/What is the Supervisor?
      1. The supervisor is often called the "highest level employee and the lowest level manager."
      2. A supervisor is a member of both management and the work group. He acts as a bridge between the two.
      3. Most problems in supervision are in the area of human relations, or people problems.
      4. Employees expect: Respect, opportunity to learn and to advance, and a sense of belonging, and so forth.
      5. Supervisors are responsible for directing people and organizing work. Planning is of paramount importance.
      6. A position description is a set of duties and responsibilities inherent to a given position.
      7. It is important to keep the position description up-to-date and to provide each employee with his own copy.

   B. The Sociology of Work
      1. People are alike in many ways; however, each individual is unique.
      2. The supervisor is challenged in getting to know employee differences. Acquiring skills in evaluating individuals is an asset.
      3. Maintaining meaningful working relationships in the organization is of great importance.
      4. The supervisor has an obligation to help individuals to develop to their fullest potential.
      5. Job rotation on a planned basis helps to build versatility and to maintain interest and enthusiasm in work groups.
      6. Cross training (job rotation) provides backup skills.

7. The supervisor can help reduce tension by maintaining a sense of humor, providing guidance to employees, and by making reasonable and timely decisions. Employees respond favorably to working under reasonably predictable circumstances.
8. Change is characteristic of all managerial behavior. The supervisor must adjust to changes in procedures, new methods, technological changes, and to a number of new and sometimes challenging situations.
9. To overcome the natural tendency for people to resist change, the supervisor should become more skillful in initiating change.

C. Principles and Practices of Supervision
1. Employees should be required to answer to only one superior.
2. A supervisor can effectively direct only a limited number of employees, depending upon the complexity, variety, and proximity of the jobs involved.
3. The organizational chart presents the organization in graphic form. It reflects lines of authority and responsibility as well as interrelationships of units within the organization.
4. Distribution of work can be improved through an analysis using the "Work Distribution Chart."
5. The "Work Distribution Chart" reflects the division of work within a unit in understandable form.
6. When related tasks are given to an employee, he has a better chance of increasing his skills through training.
7. The individual who is given the responsibility for tasks must also be given the appropriate authority to insure adequate results.
8. The supervisor should delegate repetitive, routine work. Preparation of recurring reports, maintaining leave and attendance records are some examples.
9. Good discipline is essential to good task performance. Discipline is reflected in the actions of employees on the job in the absence of supervision.
10. Disciplinary action may have to be taken when the positive aspects of discipline have failed. Reprimand, warning, and suspension are examples of disciplinary action.
11. If a situation calls for a reprimand, be sure it is deserved and remember it is to be done in private.

D. Dynamic Leadership
1. A style is a personal method or manner of exerting influence.
2. Authoritarian leaders often see themselves as the source of power and authority.
3. The democratic leader often perceives the group as the source of authority and power.
4. Supervisors tend to do better when using the pattern of leadership that is most natural for them.
5. Social scientists suggest that the effective supervisor use the leadership style that best fits the problem or circumstances involved.
6. All four styles—telling, selling, consulting, joining—have their place. Using one does not preclude using the other at another time.

7. The theory X point of view assumes that the average person dislikes work, will avoid it whenever possible, and must be coerced to achieve organizational objectives.
8. The theory Y point of view assumes that the average person considers work to be a natural as play, and, when the individual is committed, he requires little supervision or direction to accomplish desired objectives.
9. The leader's basic assumptions concerning human behavior and human nature affect his actions, decisions, and other managerial practices.
10. Dissatisfaction among employees is often present, but difficult to isolate. The supervisor should seek to weaken dissatisfaction by keeping promises, being sincere and considerate, keeping employees informed, and so forth.
11. Constructive suggestions should be encouraged during the natural progress of the work.

E. Processes for Solving Problems
1. People find their daily tasks more meaningful and satisfying when they can improve them.
2. The causes of problems, or the key factors, are often hidden in the background. Ability to solve problems often involves the ability to isolate them from their backgrounds. There is some substance to the cliché that some persons "can't see the forest for the trees."
3. New procedures are often developed from old ones. Problems should be broken down into manageable parts. New ideas can be adapted from old one.
4. People think differently in problem-solving situations. Using a logical, patterned approach is often useful. One approach found to be useful includes these steps:
   a. Define the problem
   b. Establish objectives
   c. Get the facts
   d. Weigh and decide
   e. Take action
   f. Evaluate action

F. Training for Results
1. Participants respond best when they feel training is important to them.
2. The supervisor has responsibility for the training and development of those who report to him.
3. When training is delegated to others, great care must be exercised to insure the trainer has knowledge, aptitude, and interest for his work as a trainer.
4. Training (learning) of some type goes on continually. The most successful supervisor makes certain the learning contributes in a productive manner to operational goals.
5. New employees are particularly susceptible to training. Older employees facing new job situations require specific training, as well as having need for development and growth opportunities.
6. Training needs require continuous monitoring.
7. The training officer of an agency is a professional with a responsibility to assist supervisors in solving training problems.

16

8. Many of the self-development steps important to the supervisor's own growth are equally important to the development of peers and subordinates. Knowledge of these is important when the supervisor consults with others on development and growth opportunities.

G. Health, Safety, and Accident Prevention
1. Management-minded supervisors take appropriate measures to assist employees in maintaining health and in assuring safe practices in the work environment.
2. Effective safety training and practices help to avoid injury and accidents.
3. Safety should be a management goal. All infractions of safety which are observed should be corrected without exception.
4. Employees' safety attitude, training and instruction, provision of safe tools and equipment, supervision, and leadership are considered highly important factors which contribute to safety and which can be influenced directly by supervisors.
5. When accidents do occur, they should be investigated promptly for very important reasons, including the fact that information which is gained can be used to prevent accidents in the future.

H. Equal Employment Opportunity
1. The supervisor should endeavor to treat all employees fairly, without regard to religion, race, sex, or national origin.
2. Groups tend to reflect the attitude of the leader. Prejudice can be detected even in very subtle form. Supervisors must strive to create a feeling of mutual respect and confidence in every employee.
3. Complete utilization of all human resources is a national goal. Equitable consideration should be accorded women in the work force, minority-group members, the physically and mentally handicapped, and the older employee. The important question is: "Who can do the job?"
4. Training opportunities, recognition for performance, overtime assignments, promotional opportunities, and all other personnel actions are to be handled on an equitable basis.

I. Improving Communications
1. Communications is achieving understanding between the sender and the receiver of a message. It also means sharing information—the creation of understanding.
2. Communication is basic to all human activity. Words are means of conveying meanings; however, real meanings are in people.
3. There are very practical differences in the effectiveness of one-way, impersonal, and two-way communications. Words spoken face-to-face are better understood. Telephone conversations are effective, but lack the rapport of person-to-person exchanges. The whole person communicates.
4. Cooperation and communication in an organization go hand in hand. When there is a mutual respect between people, spelling out rules and procedures for communicating is unnecessary.
5. There are several barriers to effective communications. These include failure to listen with respect and understanding, lack of skill in feedback, and misinterpreting the meanings of words used by the speaker. It is also common

practice to listen to what we want to hear, and tune out things we do not want to hear.
6. Communication is management's chief problem. The supervisor should accept the challenge to communicate more effectively and to improve interagency and intra-agency communications.
7. The supervisor may often plan for and conduct meetings. The planning phase is critical and may determine the success or the failure of a meeting.
8. Speaking before groups usually requires extra effort. Stage fright may never disappear completely, but it can be controlled.

J. Self-Development
1. Every employee is responsible for his own self-development.
2. Toastmaster and toastmistress clubs offer opportunities to improve skills in oral communications.
3. Planning for one's own self-development is of vital importance. Supervisors know their own strengths and limitations better than anyone else.
4. Many opportunities are open to aid the supervisor in his developmental efforts, including job assignments; training opportunities, both governmental and non-governmental—to include universities and professional conferences and seminars.
5. Programmed instruction offers a means of studying at one's own rate.
6. Where difficulties may arise from a supervisor's being away from his work for training, he may participate in televised home study or correspondence courses to meet his self-development needs.

K. Teaching and Training
1. The Teaching Process
Teaching is encouraging and guiding the learning activities of students toward established goals. In most cases this process consists of five steps: preparation, presentation, summarization, evaluation, and application.

   a. Preparation
   Preparation is two-fold in nature; that of the supervisor and the employee. Preparation by the supervisor is absolutely essential to success. He must know what, when, where, how, and whom he will teach. Some of the factors that should be considered are:
   1) The objectives
   2) The materials needed
   3) The methods to be used
   4) Employee participation
   5) Employee interest
   6) Training aids
   7) Evaluation
   8) Summarization

   Employee preparation consists in preparing the employee to receive the material. Probably the most important single factor in the preparation of the employee is arousing and maintaining his interest. He must know the objectives of the training, why he is there, how the material can be used, and its importance to him.

b. Presentation
   In presentation, have a carefully designed plan and follow it. The plan should be accurate and complete, yet flexible enough to meet situations as they arise. The method of presentation will be determined by the particular situation and objectives.

c. Summary
   A summary should be made at the end of every training unit and program. In addition, there may be internal summaries depending on the nature of the material being taught. The important thing is that the trainee must always be able to understand how each part of the new material relates to the whole.

d. Application
   The supervisor must arrange work so the employee will be given a chance to apply new knowledge or skills while the material is still clear in his mind and interest is high. The trainee does not really know whether he has learned the material until he has been given a chance to apply it. If the material is not applied, it loses most of its value.

e. Evaluation
   The purpose of all training is to promote learning. To determine whether the training has been a success or failure, the supervisor must evaluate this learning.
   In the broadest sense, evaluation includes all the devices, methods, skills, and techniques used by the supervisor to keep himself and the employees informed as to their progress toward the objectives they are pursuing. The extent to which the employee has mastered the knowledge, skills, and abilities, or changed his attitudes, as determined by the program objectives, is the extent to which instruction has succeeded or failed.
   Evaluation should not be confined to the end of the lesson, day, or program but should be used continuously. We shall note later the way this relates to the rest of the teaching process.

2. Teaching Methods
   A teaching method is a pattern of identifiable student and instructor activity used in presenting training material.
   All supervisors are faced with the problem of deciding which method should be used at a given time.

   a. Lecture
      The lecture is direct oral presentation of material by the supervisor. The present trend is to place less emphasis on the trainer's activity and more on that of the trainee.

   b. Discussion
      Teaching by discussion or conference involves using questions and other techniques to arouse interest and focus attention upon certain areas, and by doing so creating a learning situation. This can be one of the most

valuable methods because it gives the employees an opportunity to express their ideas and pool their knowledge.

c. Demonstration
The demonstration is used to teach how something works or how to do something. It can be used to show a principle or what the results of a series of actions will be. A well-staged demonstration is particularly effective because it shows proper methods of performance in a realistic manner.

d. Performance
Performance is one of the most fundamental of all learning techniques or teaching methods. The trainee may be able to tell how a specific operation should be performed but he cannot be sure he knows how to perform the operation until he has done so.
As with all methods, there are certain advantages and disadvantages to each method.

e. Which Method to Use
Moreover, there are other methods and techniques of teaching. It is difficult to use any method without other methods entering into it. In any learning situation, a combination of methods is usually more effective than any one method alone.

Finally, evaluation must be integrated into the other aspects of the teaching-learning process.

It must be used in the motivation of the trainees; it must be used to assist in developing understanding during the training; and it must be related to employee application of the results of training.

This is distinctly the role of the supervisor.